M000290646

THE 12 THINGS THEY WANTED TO TEACH YOU IN HIGH SCHOOL...BUT COULDN'T

PRAISE

FOR THE 12 THINGS THEY WANTED TO TEACH YOU IN HIGH SCHOOL...BUT COULDN'T

"Loved reading it!"
- **Jeff Martin**, *CEO, University Recruiters; 2020 Yahoo Finance Top CEO's*

"High school was a wonderful experience for me. I had the opportunity to grow as a student and learn the necessary skillsets in order to achieve success from a higher education perspective. What I didn't learn was how to cope with stress, manage failure to the best of my ability, and how to take care of my body from a nutritional standpoint. I wish I'd had *The 12 Things They Wanted to Teach You in High School...But Couldn't* at my disposal then. This book is a blueprint and gift that will enhance the success rate of the younger generation!"
- **Paul Carcaterra**, *ESPN*

"*The 12 Things They Wanted to Teach You in High School...But Couldn't* is a truly intentional resource that is a summation of successes and failures of the individuals who came before us. Please take this knowledge and apply it as a rule and guide."
- **Rashaad Pitt**, *High School Assistant Principal*

"Education is so much more than content. By the time I entered graduate school, my mind was full of facts about science and math. However, I quickly realized I was very limited in my coping skills. I struggled to deal with setbacks,

thinking it was a sign of weakness to ask for help. Looking back, I wish I had learned these skills at a much younger age. The powerful words in The 12 Things They Wanted to Teach You In High School...But Couldn't spotlight the importance of learning by experience and example and the value of knowing and loving yourself—something every impressionable young teen should be given the opportunity to do. The book is a perfect reminder that as the world is changing, so should our educational system."
- **Tracy Degl,** *Special Education Teacher*

"As a teacher, Rob inspires me with his vibrance and messaging. He has listened deeply to the voices of educators, principals, athletes, and coaches—folks young and old. His message in this book can be summed up in this quote: *"My heart, and the heart of this book, is to speak to your conscience."* Ultimately, the journey to self is a journey of listening; and, while sometimes it's hard to hear ourselves, his voice comes through loud and clear. Rob is here to help you hear yourself."
- **Andrea Rossin,** *High School Teacher*

ISBN

978-1-0879-2603-2 (Hardcover)

978-1-0879-2857-9 (EPUB)

1 - EDUCATION / Professional Development

2 - EDUCATION / Administration / General

3 - EDUCATION / Educational Psychology

Distributed to the trade by The Ingram Book Company

THE 12 THINGS THEY WANTED TO TEACH YOU IN HIGH SCHOOL...BUT COULDN'T

A PERSONAL DEVELOPMENT BOOK FOR EDUCATIONAL LEADERS

BY

ROBERT ANDERSON, JR.

TO MY WIFE KELLY...

...who has given us an amazing family and who takes risks with
me every day that allow me to chase my dreams. I pray I can help
you achieve yours.

CONTENTS

CONTENTS

THANK YOU...

Mom, Dad, Nana, and Papa.

The only way I can show you how much I appreciate what you've taught me is to share the gifts you've given me with the world.

THANK YOU... Mike, Amy, E.R. and Aunt Barbara—you taught me what family first is. I won't let you down.

THANK YOU...to my teachers. Mr. Brogan for your humor; Mr. McCracken for your smoke jumping-stories; Ms. Ellen Mager for your intensity— you're the first woman athlete, coach, and teacher I met that wanted to **WIN** all the time! I can't tell you how that shaped my perception of female athletes as a high school kid.

THANK YOU... Mr. Longobardi for taking a risk on an overly confident new teacher with no experience. I know I was a handful to have on staff. Teaching under your leadership was a major highlight of my career.

THANK YOU...to my coaches:

Mr. Allen Anderson, my first football coach. Coach Santavicca, the lifeline, heart, and soul of my high school athletic career—you're the standard; enough said! Mitch Lieberman, you kept me in the game as a coach—your faith, confidence, and love helped skyrocket my coaching career and helped me to be seen as an equal at the high school level. Coach Simpson, for believing in me as a college athlete. Coach Ford, for always jogging down to the practice field and setting the tone with your energy, preparation, and attention to detail.

THANK YOU...to all of the families that entrusted me with their daughters and sons as a trainer, coach, and teacher. I want you to know I never took your trust lightly.

THANK YOU...to my wingman Karl Danny J. I love you! I miss you! I will always carry your legacy in my heart. You're my brother, my best friend, my best man, my confidant, my selfless warrior. I wouldn't be me without you.

THANK YOU...to all of the athletes that trained at 5:30 am, trained under car lights on grass fields, worked out in freezing cold garages, took cold plunges with me, ran the park with me during snowstorms, froze on turf fields during winter weather advisories, ran sprints in rainstorms and heavy winds, carried 100-plus pound logs with me out of the woods. (Part of me is grateful social media wasn't a thing early on in my career)... You know who you are! Your intensity and commitment inspired me daily!

MY DAILY INSPIRATION... Anderson children Javon, Payton, Cadyn, and Mathias; my heart and soul cries when I think someone may mistreat you because of the color of your skin. I hope this book touches the hearts of those who have been misled and empowers people of influence to take action to protect you.

#THEYCANTSEEMYDREAMS

DARE TO DREAM BIG

LET'S GO!

WHO WILL BE SERVED BY READING THIS BOOK?

This book will serve you well if you're interested in teaching, currently teaching, or have a desire to change our broken educational system.

This book will serve you well if you were a student in a traditional educational system. Odds are, when you graduated you didn't know who you were as a person. Odds are you weren't taught how to set goals, how to create the right nutritional program to keep you healthy, or why it's important to have conversations about race and social injustice and learn about the pain and struggle that people of color have experienced.

If you went through a traditional educational system and didn't learn those things, odds are the well-intended educators in our schools didn't learn them either.

If our educators didn't learn those skills in high school, college, or graduate school, how can we expect them to teach those skills to our kids?

Our kids spend 6-7 hours a day, 180 days a year, for 13 years—an average of 14,000 hours of opportunities our educators have to serve—and the most important issues of our time are being ignored!

We can't go back and change our experiences, but we can create new opportunities for our kids.

This is a personal development book written to serve educational leaders, parents, and community members that know we're missing something but don't know what or where to start.

WHO IS KARL DANNY...?

Growing up, I had the opportunity to meet and experience life with my soul brother—you know, that person that makes you look good because they're so good!

SO FUNNY!

SO LOVING!

SO GOOD LOOKING!

ALWAYS WELCOMING!

NEVER INTIMIDATING!

You know, that person in your life that protects your blind spots with love and encouragement—that person that will never let you feel dumb for your actions or mistakes.

He was the guy telling you to drive past his house at the end of the night because he's concerned about you getting home safely. Karl Danny would routinely drive home with me to my house an hour outside of Manhattan, spend the night, then take the train back to the Bronx in the morning. All this because he needed to make sure I got home safely each night. He was always looking out for me.

That's the role Karl Danny played in my life.

And...we had a plan!

When I was done with school and athletics, he was going to move out of the Bronx and join me in the suburbs to raise our families together.

We had many things in common—but Danny was a city kid, and I was a suburban kid. My idea of playing was jumping on my bike, having a catch in the yard, or running hills for an hour.

His idea of playing was hitting the video games and walking to the corner for a slice of pizza.

I wanted to run sprints; he had girls running after him!

I was 220 pounds, lived in the weight room, and looked like I'd just walked out of a horror movie. He was 150 pounds, baby-faced, with a smooth grin and infectious level of swag that would leave you feeling good for days.

We were the perfect blend of beauty and the beast. I'll let you guess who the beast was...

One day he called me while I was at school, two weeks before Halloween. He told me the city is always crazy around Halloween and said he should spend the weekend with me.

I told him absolutely, do it, and to drive up anytime. We also needed to celebrate his new entry-level position at an accounting firm that he was all fired up about.

But we never reconnected about him coming up to visit.

Then, on what seemed like a random Wednesday night, my mom showed up at my college house.

I was so excited and surprised. I was thinking, a home-cooked meal on a Wednesday—LET'S GO! I immediately handed over the reins in the kitchen and let my mom finish cooking.

It was odd that she was there, though, because I had just seen her over the weekend at my last football game. But it wasn't that odd. She's so crazy she would tell me she just happened to be in the neighborhood and wanted to visit—from a two-hour drive away!

Then she turned to me as she was cooking and said, "Danny got hurt on Halloween night."

There was something in her eyes. The first question I managed to ask was, "Did he make it...?"

She told me that as he was driving to a Halloween party, kids started throwing eggs at his car. He stopped and jumped out to say, "Enough."

Before he could get back in, someone drunk and high walked out of a nearby house and shot him in the head.

He died on the scene with his girlfriend in the front seat.

I never had a best man at my wedding.

I never had a bachelor party.

I never celebrated his new job.

I never bought a house in the suburbs with my wingman living down the street.

I never got to see Karl Danny live his dreams.

My friend, I celebrate you through one of my greatest passions... EDUCATION.

Together we will create educators who embody everything you represented.

Self-Aware – Curious – Empathetic

Your legacy lives on in my heart and actions.

Now your name will live on as well by improving the lives of our educators around the world.

I hope I'm making you smile!

LETS BEGIN OUR EDUCATIONAL RENOVATION...

...by pouring into the people that give our kids the most: our teachers!

I'm going to share 12 of the most impactful things you can do to improve your quality of life so you can become more self-aware, empathetic, and curious about life.

Here's a list of the 12 Things you will be introduced to that will change your life, reinvent how you teach, and start our educational renovation...

1) LOVE AND INCLUSION

...Healing the hearts, minds, anger, fear, and pain caused by racism and injustice.

2) HOW TO IDENTIFY YOUR GIFTS

...Learning how to define and apply your gift.

3) OVERCOMING DOUBT

...All achievers have doubt, but you can push past it.

4) FEELING ANXIOUS...NOW WHAT?

...Shifting your focus to shift your emotion.

5) ANXIETY IS HERE...NOW WHAT?

...Transforming your anxiety into power.

6) YES, YOU CAN CREATE THE LIFE YOU WANT...EVEN IF YOU'RE STARTING LATER

...Education can evolve, and so can you. I will show you how.

7) CONFIDENCE IS CREATED; YOU AREN'T BORN WITH IT

...Staying confidently connected to your passion.

8) IT'S MY BODY; NOW IT'S TIME TO RECLAIM IT

...Your health, your life, your body–let's take control.

9) THE SECRET IS TO CREATE A MISSION, NOT TO JUST FOLLOW YOUR PASSION

...Your mission will create clarity and power, because passion isn't enough.

10) WHY AN ATHLETIC MINDSET WILL HELP YOU ACHIEVE EVERYTHING YOU WANT

...How winners win.

11) FOUNDATIONAL PRINCIPLES OF NUTRITION

...Building a healthy and impactful nutritional program doesn't start with food.

12) RECOVERING FROM DEATH AND GRIEVING

...Losing our caregivers is a stage in our journey–how to create a life worth living in their honor.

When you feel good about your life—about your decision to become a teacher or administrator—your positive energy and renewed sense of self will be contagious with your students and staff.

When your fears, opinions, and concerns about students in your school can be turned into curiosity, we will be on our way to healing the hearts of the underserved and enlightening the minds of the privileged.

―――――――

AT THE HEART OF THIS BOOK:

My heart, and the heart of this book, is to speak to your conscience.

This book will share how you can become a KarlDanny Educator that will feel empowered to positively influence our schools and communities...

SELF-AWARE + EMPATHETIC + CURIOUS = THE KARLDANNY EDUCATOR

We need to change our educational system. The challenge in changing our educational system is...it takes time! A LOT of time! 50 years is the average time it takes to implement a new national standard in America.

Even so, *methodologies for improvement* can be applied overnight.

KarlDanny Educator is a system that I have applied as a classroom teacher, a lacrosse coach, and an athletic performance trainer. I've shared it with thousands of families that I have advised and/or spoken in front of over the last two decades.

If our educators are going to have an opportunity to make impactful changes with students—that are relevant today—we need a shift in conscience that will allow our students to apply what they're learning and experiencing.

A KarlDanny Educator will challenge and teach you how to improve your intrapersonal skills. When we create students that have a stronger sense of self, they'll be less likely to be persuaded by negativity, hate, and divisive behavior.

Students that wake up knowing what their purpose is in the world, and have a mission to support their passion, won't need to break the law, skip school, and recklessly experiment with drugs. They will start to find out how to share their voice with the world.

Implementing the KarlDanny Education System will empower students to become curious again. They'll ask questions in class, solve simple and complex problems, and tap into the GRIT everyone has inside of them.

Educating our K-12 students on the importance of anti-racism and social injustice is a necessity. It's one of the steps forward we haven't taken within the educational system.

We have plenty of examples in history when laws were changed but equality wasn't.

After the church bombing in 1964 that killed four black children, the Civil Rights Act was signed into law. If simply changing laws worked, why then do we still have a tremendous amount of social unrest in the United States?

The infamous War on Drugs—supported in the 1980s and 90s by the Reagan (R) and Clinton (D) administrations, respectively—was responsible for placing a disproportionate number of Black men in jail for non-violent crimes. We're still experiencing an unconscionable level of social unrest between the police and the Black and Brown communities.

If we don't have a shift in consciousness as a society—and then teach our students how to shift their consciousness—nothing is ever going to change in education.

Our teachers have the ability. We have to share a system they can adopt, support them through the implementation process, and allow them to be creative through the process.

Instead of waiting for state and local officials to make changes to our curriculum, we have an opportunity to demand change on a massive level right now. We're living in a time of such massive uncertainty due to Covid-19. Now is the time for our educators to create new systems that disrupt our current educational format.

Perhaps a new system of educating our school-aged kids could have prevented the tragedies we've seen in recent history—from the murder of George Floyd by a police officer, to the mass killings in Nigeria, to discovering a way to prevent the wildfires in California from getting progressively worse every year.

If we change the conversations we're having in our schools, allow students to find their voice prior to graduation, offer our educators solutions to their biggest fears, and teach students how to build authentic connections...

...The result will be that students will become more **SELF-AWARE, EMPATHETIC, AND CURIOUS!**

A KarlDanny Educator knows how to keep their cup of empowerment full. Empowered teachers create empowered students.

I know everything starts with a student's home life. I'm fully aware that a student's town and history is going to impact their view on society—either seeing it more positively or negatively depending on the context.

The good thing is that negative views can improve over time with the right influences. But why should we have to unlearn behaviors and viewpoints that don't serve us if we can get right to the root of the problem through sound educational practices that serve the current needs of our students and staff?

WE have an opportunity in education to teach to the heart of students. We may not be part of a student's home life, but more than 500 million students walk through the doors of our high schools around the world. *The 12 Things They Wanted to Teach You in High School...But Couldn't* speaks to the heart of teachers and ignites the spirit they started this profession with.

Perhaps one day we will be able to stand at the podium for our high school graduates and say they found their inner voice and that they're ready to share it proudly with the world.

———

OVER THE LAST TWENTY YEARS I have been regarded as one of the best team builders you've never heard of that grew up in Yorktown, NY.

I would consider myself a good athlete, not exceptional. I had to work for every inch of my athletic accomplishments. I would consider myself to be a great teacher, not exceptional. There are people far more intelligent than I in the profession. I would consider myself to be a very good personal trainer and lacrosse coach, not all-knowing. There are people in the field who have a level of insight I aspire to achieve.

But, I know I'm an exceptional team builder!

If you're going to build a team you need to know how to meet their needs. Before you can meet their needs, you need to know how to influence and empower people.

...AND

Get results....

For more than 30 years I have studied, read, and listened to people I consider to be the most influential voices in the world. I've taken their voices and expertise and poured it into the high school and college-aged students I've worked with for the last twenty years.

I'm going to share how our school leadership, parents, and students can improve their ability to recognize each other's needs and how they can improve communication between students, parents, and school staff.

I'm also going to do a deep dive into the personal psychology of high school and college-aged young adults.

High school students don't want to be alone; they want to feel part of something bigger than themselves.

Educators don't go into the profession because they hate kids—so why should we settle for less than their students' greatness? It's time to come together and design a curriculum that meets the needs of our students and honors the creativity and talents of our teachers.

That's in part what fuels me to share this book and the methodology of a KarlDanny Educator.

Our schools are in desperate need of a curriculum renovation. Instead of waiting for the state to make changes, we can make micro changes at the local level that will lead to a massive shift in the way our kids think and approach life.

That's my why...

12 Things They Wanted to Teach You in High School...But Couldn't is everything I have been teaching in the classroom, on the athletic field, and as a consultant. It builds teams and communities, enhances individual talent, enhances the abilities of our educators, and supports them to become more **SELF-AWARE, EMPATHETIC, AND CURIOUS.**

Personal development for our educators is one of the only ways to help us create students that are 21st century ready when they graduate from high school.

This is the secret sauce every leader, parent, teacher, and school administrator can use to change the culture of their town, community, and school building.

ONE DAY YOUR LIFE AND IMPACT IS GOING TO FLASH BEFORE YOUR EYES—MAKE SURE ITS WORTH WATCHING!

Enjoy, learn, grow, and...

GET READY TO FINALLY BECOME PART OF THE SOLUTION THAT WILL CHANGE THE WORLD...

THE POWER OF GOAL SETTING

THE FOUNDATION OF PERSONAL DEVELOPMENT

ONE OF THE MOST IMPORTANT aspects of achievement is learning how to set goals...so much so that if you research goal setting, you'll find books, speeches, classes, videos, masterminds, and speakers all focused on teaching goal setting.

Goal setting should be the foundation of our educational system.

WHY?

Because it works!

Odds are you didn't take a class, or have anyone in school talk to you about the power of goal setting.

It's time to start asking our educational leaders—at the state and local levels—why teachers don't have the tools they need to teach one of the most powerful skills in long-term achievement. This is the first step we need to take to create a KarlDanny educator!

To achieve a high level of happiness and fulfillment we have to be intentional. When life starts happening, you aren't going to just be happy. It certainly isn't anyone's else responsibility to make you happy. You will need to set goals and become intentional about creating experiences. It's those experiences that will lead you to feel fulfilled and joyful.

You will certainly have to set goals if you're interested in achieving a high level of fulfillment academically and professionally. Again, it isn't going to just happen.

Why do we have more young people taking their own life at an earlier and earlier age? Why do we have a historical number of adults on anti-depressants, taking illegal drugs, and using food as an anti-anxiety drug instead of exercise.

The answer is, in large part, because our educational system isn't preparing kids for the world we're living in today.

WHY DO WE SET GOALS?

Because it works…Get clear on what you want, write it down, set a timeline, review it daily, and execute.

Here's a formula I've adapted from Jim Rohn, one of the original personal development speakers in the United States…

His work is legendary. I think his formula is a brilliant place to start your journey of learning what you should have learned in high school about goal setting but didn't!

Step 1: Write down the five things you're proud of accomplishing (let's get momentum).

Step 2: Write down 30-50 things you would like to accomplish over the next 10 years (this is a critical step, take the time to complete this exercise and everything else is going to fall into place). Here's a list of questions to help you complete your list...

- What experiences would you like to have?

- Who would you like to meet?

- How much money would you like to have in the bank in 10 years?

- Describe your health 10 years from now?

Step 3: Mark each goal with a 1, 3, 5, or 10 that will indicate how many years you think you'll need to accomplish each goal (most people don't have enough things on their list of accomplishments that will take 10 years. Typically, the majority of goals people have are short-sighted...**THINK BIG!**).

"WE OVERESTIMATE WHAT WE CAN ACCOMPLISH IN A YEAR, AND UNDERESTIMATE WHAT WE CAN ACCOMPLISH IN A DECADE." -TONY ROBBINS

Step 4: Create a top-four list from your list of goals (things that will absolutely give your life meaning).

Step 5: Explain why you want to accomplish each goal on your top-four list.

Step 6: What makes you feel alive? Do more of that every week (know thyself).

Step 7: What makes you feel like you're dying Inside? Stay away from this (know thyself).

Step 8: REVIEW daily.

Step 9: EXECUTE.

Do yourself a favor…apply the principles of goal setting to your life. Before you teach Rohn's method, I want to encourage you as the educators to apply his method of goal setting to your own routine. When you apply his method of goal setting to your life and vision for the future…you'll begin to feel as though you're growing and expanding as a professional. Watch how the world will reveal itself to you.

WHAT IF YOU HIT 80% OF EVERYTHING ON YOUR LIST OF GOALS?

That's the national average for people that write their goals down, review them daily, and execute. You could potentially accomplish 8 out of every 10 things on your list within the next 10 years.

Wouldn't that be an amazing 10 years of living?

Don't you think that would set you on a course to living a meaningful and fulfilled life?

Sounds simple; simple isn't always easy! Because it's so easy, people don't do it! However, if you're reading this book…you don't want to be average!

You've already come this far, let's go! It's time to start living. It's time to start feeling fulfilled and having a sense of accomplishment and contribution!

Don't waste another day!

LET'S GO!

"BE INSPIRED TO TAKE IMPERFECT ACTION!"

"I WISH AMERICANS LOVED BLACK PEOPLE AS MUCH AS THEY LOVE BLACK CULTURE." -JALEN ROSE

1) LOVE AND INCLUSION

LOVE IS IN THE HEART. It's the source of inspiration, connection, community, and positive growth. We all want to experience these things in one way or another, and love points the way.

So why, then, do we still find so many people that choose hate rather than love, choosing to adopt attitudes of racism, injustice, and other forms of discrimination?

Racism clouds the heart. Racism can be defined as how someone negatively feels about an individual of another race without knowing them.

Injustice inflames the heart. Injustice is how someone acts negatively towards another person.

Racism and injustice are two different things, though oftentimes they're used interchangeably.

I would like to begin this chapter by attempting to appeal to your heart in hopes of you seeing the injustice that's taken place around the world. My hope is you'll feel filled with a burning desire to take immediate action to help cure our society.

If I can appeal to your heart, perhaps you'll feel empowered to say something to friends, colleagues, and family. Hopefully, if you're taking action, you will continue to take action and heal the hearts of the people in your social circles that don't believe social injustice is their issue, or just don't see it.

The murder of George Floyd took place at the knee of Police Officer Derek Chauvin on May 25th, 2020, in Minneapolis, Minnesota. It caused the world to reevaluate how comfortable we are with death.

...How comfortable we are with murder!

...How comfortable we are with police officers taking advantage of their position of authority.

My dad wanted me to follow in his footsteps and become a police officer. When I was a kid I remember feeling as though my dad protected the universe. Then my uncles became officers and sheriffs. Being an officer seemed to by my destiny.

I didn't ultimately choose law enforcement for a career. Even so, my respect and admiration for the position hasn't changed.

I know that there are good cops out there—but it's been clear for decades that there are officers that abuse their power.

"THERE COMES A TIME WHEN SILENCE IS BETRAYAL." -MARTIN LUTHER KING, JR.

The murder of George Floyd is significant because it was the first time that our white friends and brothers believed that we as Black and Brown people are under attack—and have been continuously under attack for hundreds, if not thousands of years. After all, slavery dates back as far as ancient Sumer—around 3500 BC— and as early as the 1400s when slavery was present in what would later become America.

Unfortunately, injustice in the United States is the reality at the moment.

George Floyd's murder wasn't a wake-up call for Black and Brown people—we live the reality of being wrongfully judged and feeling hunted (at times) on a daily basis. I pray his murder was an awakening for our White friends, neighbors, colleagues and family members.

I believe in people, and I believe people are good. Now is the time to express it. When you're a good person, the tendency isn't to walk around telling everyone you're a good person.

When you're a racist, you exploit your opportunities when they're presented.

My appeal is to the majority: we (America and the World) need you to share your heart, your LOVE!

1) It starts at Home. Talk to your kids about what you believe— don't assume they know. Our kids are being bombarded with mixed messages like everyone else in the world. They need to hear from you and know where you stand. One conversation isn't enough.

2) Say Hello. I have endured countless times when people have crossed the street when they see me coming. Stepped off the elevator when I walk on or hugged their kids tight when I walked by. Say hello—positive energy is contagious.

3) Share your view when "friends" decide to pass judgment and hate. If you aren't part of the solution, you're part of the problem. Silence is compliance.

When we cry out that we're being treated unfairly, or take a knee during the national anthem (Colin Kaepernick) to bring awareness to the systematic oppression of Black and Brown people…

...We're crying out because WE NEED HELP.

WE love our country.

WE respect police officers.

WE want our kids to live.

WE believe that all lives matter.

Right now, Black lives are under attack...

George Floyd's murder was filmed and broadcasted around the world on social media outlets at a time when the world wasn't distracted. Because of Covid-19, everyone was home, with nowhere to go. We were glued to our devices, Netflix, and board games...

The moment he was murdered it became undeniable...

...that he was alive when the officers arrived.

...that he was dying on film at the knee of the arresting officers.

...that he knew he was dying, as he called out for his deceased mother moments before he took his last breath.

The reality is, those officers may have never been told they're racist. Their supervisors may have never been taught not to be racist, or how to identify racism and racist acts.

At some point, someone taught them to be racist. Someone taught them to hate Black and Brown people. Someone taught them to kill us if they have a chance.

"I LEARNED THAT COURAGE WAS NOT THE ABSENCE OF FEAR, BUT THE TRIUMPH OVER IT. THE BRAVE MAN IS NOT HE WHO DOES NOT FEEL AFRAID, BUT HE WHO CONQUERS THAT FEAR." -NELSON MANDELA

Georges Floyd's murder being caught on tape has caused the world to reevaluate humanity. I believe one of the places our humanity needs to be addressed is in our school system.

I have personally experienced the beauty of people and educators during my time as a student and a teacher.

I have also experienced frustration, embarrassment, and have been subjected to stereotypical behavior that made me feel singled out and lonely. When I reflect back on those moments, I know I'm not alone. I ask that you please allow this list to serve as a reminder that Black and Brown kids don't enjoy being singled out and asked to explain their "blackness."

Can I touch your hair?

How do you clean your skin?

You only got into that school to fill a quota!

You aren't Black enough!

All Black kids can play basketball!

You can't swim!

I know you like fried chicken!

Wow, you speak so well, in grammatically correct sentences! You dress so nice, not like those other kids!

Wait, you have a mom AND a dad at home?!

I've personally had all of these phrases said to me by teachers and/or students—and I'm not unique.

If you've said these things—or heard someone else say these things but didn't step in and say something—you aren't being curious; you're showing every Black and Brown person that you're ignorant to the reality of how these phrases are making us feel.

"THE ENEMY IS FEAR. WE THINK IT IS HATE, BUT IT IS FEAR." -MAHATMA GANDHI

Our educational leaders have a lot of responsibly; it can take decades to officially change things at the state level. We have a responsibility to humanity to take action right now at the local level.

Speak to your school leaders—superintendents, principals, and union presidents.

Ask them to prioritize conversations of inclusion and create a task force focused on creating a curriculum to teach our kids how to love and be inclusive in their actions and words. The task force should have the ability to bring in consultants and speakers who can help create digestible resources for the teachers and administrators to implement.

The responsibility of the task force should be to create a curriculum that speaks to the needs of the unheard voices in school. Members of our Latino community, LGBTQ community, and other minority groups represented in your school district.

Pain has a voice…

As educators, it's our responsibility to ask underrepresented groups how they're being treated in school and within the community. Their pain has a voice, and we need to provide them with an outlet and education to share their experiences.

If we aren't going to teach our kids that racism is wrong, someone is going to teach them it's right.

"I BELIEVE THAT NOW IS FINALLY THE TIME."

CONVERSATIONS

Having conversations about love and inclusion—and the perils of discrimination in all of its forms—is the most important aspect of eliminating racism and injustice from the heart once and for all.

As we're thinking about taking on a massive task such as racism in our communities and schools, I would like to shift your mindset from racism and injustice to LOVE and INCLUSION!

Here's the truth: I'm exhausted thinking about racism and re-living the times I have been subjected to racism.

My exhaustion comes from feeling that we haven't made enough progress. When I look at the times we're living in, I have a renewed sense of excitement. I know we have a chance to make lasting change happen right now!

Our educational leaders need to provide our kids with opportunities to learn the truth about our past. And as we move forward, we need to be a shining example of LOVE and INCLUSION.

When I think about LOVE I think about how my family showed their love to each other when I was in school.

We ate traditional meals together.

We traveled together.

Everyone was responsible for something in the house.

When we had problems, we figured it out together.

If you want to teach students how to be more EMPATHETIC and LOVING in school, please don't make it complicated.

Start by thinking about how you would create a positive atmosphere with your family, then create that atmosphere in your school or classroom.

If you can't use your family as a reference point due to your upbringing, seek out support to guide you (something I cover in full in a later chapter). If you want to create a family atmosphere you'll have to be intentional—it isn't going to just happen.

INCLUSION

You don't need to wear a shirt or post a sticker on your door to prove that you're inclusive. Those things are nice and certainly feel good to see, but creating an inclusive atmosphere begins by asking questions. Ask your students about...

...their likes and dislikes related to food, sports, travel locations, musical artists.

...how they spend their time away from school.

...how they celebrate their victories and reflect on missed opportunities.

Share a moment of vulnerability about yourself and have the courage to laugh about it.

As an educational leader think about moments that made you feel welcome and re-create those in your building and classroom.

"INJUSTICE ANYWHERE IS A THREAT TO JUSTICE EVERYWHERE" -MARTIN LUTHER KING, JR.

The names below have been murdered by police, died in police custody for no good reason, found hung in a tree and had their death ruled a suicide, or mysteriously disappeared:

George Floyd, Eric Garner, Tamir Rice, Michael Brown, Sandra Bland, Ezell Ford, Dante Parker, Michelle Cusseaux, Laquan McDonald, Tanisha Anderson, Akai Gurley, Rumain Brisbon, Jerame Reid, George Mann, Matthew Ajibade, Frank Smart, Breonna Taylor, John Crawford III, Natasha McKenna, Tony Robinson, Mya Hall, Walter Scott, Amani Kildea, Tony McDade

I'm sharing these names with you in hopes of imploring you to take action. My name, or the name of my kids, could easily be added to that list.

Law enforcement is one area of our communities that needs to be improved. At some point, every officer was someone's student. Every officer sat in a classroom and had the opportunity to be taught why it's important to be inclusive, why it's important to see the world through the eyes of curiosity, empathy, and love.

Our relationship with law enforcement isn't the only place we can focus efforts. But it can make the difference between life and death if those people trained in the use of lethal force direct it in ways that are ill-informed!

Creating love and inclusion in our schools is one of the most important steps we need to take action towards as a nation and around the world. If our young students are trained this way early on, they can carry that wisdom with them into any career they choose later on.

Having the courage to create LOVE and INCLUSION in our communities needs to become our mission. But creating a loving and inclusive community isn't one socioeconomic group's responsibility.

The mission—along with the conversations about inclusion— needs to be adopted in the wealthiest parts of the world, in the finest schools, as well as in underdeveloped areas.

We're living in a time where our youth believe it's our job (Black, White, and Brown) to change the inequalities of the world. Our youth are taking matters into their own hands and demanding change.

We have to have the courage to start having these conversations in our communities, uncover our biased beliefs, and share how we can create positive multicultural experiences.

It isn't complicated. It starts by speaking to your family, friends, and students about your beliefs and passions.

The opportunities to create a new mission will present themselves when you take the first step and share your views on why we need to be more inclusive and purposeful in sharing our love.

I believe people are good. I believe in the human spirit.

I believe that my kids will have an opportunity to grow up in a country that doesn't predetermine if they're a super-predator, a convict, or a threat before they speak or have a chance to introduce themselves.

I believe this is the generation that won't stand for a lack of love and inclusion and will finally vote for humanity over everything.

I believe that now is finally the time!

RECAP: CREATING A KARLDANNY EDUCATOR

- It's the source of inspiration, connection, community, and positive growth. We all want to experience these things in one way or another, and love points the way.

- Racism clouds the heart. It's how someone feels about another individual person without knowing them.

- Injustice inflames the heart. Injustice is how someone acts negatively towards another person.

- Choose to teach from the perspective of LOVE and INCLUSION instead of racism and injustice. When you take that perspective, it should open your heart and mind.

- You aren't curious when you ask the Black and Brown community to justify our "blackness" by explaining our kinky hair or our light brown skin color.

- Creating a community that focuses on love and inclusion is the key to changing how we communicate with each other and put our conscious and unconscious biases away. Having a desire to address racism will give us a chance to overcome it.

- Self-education and courage are the keys to having uncomfortable but necessary conversations.

"YOUR GIFT IS THE THING THAT YOU DO BEST THAT REQUIRES THE LEAST AMOUNT OF EFFORT."
-STEVE HARVEY

2) HOW TO IDENTIFY YOUR GIFTS

THE WORLD HAS CHANGED SINCE I was a kid.

Students are more interested and vocal about learning from *people* that are currently winning in real life than they are in studying the theory and concepts that traditional learning methods in schools promote.

I agree with the movement!

I'm pro teacher!

I'm pro education!

We need to evolve; the evolution begins by pouring into our educators. By helping our educators become the best version of themselves we will have an opportunity to move our students.

43

If you want to move someone's heart and spirit, you have to be moved. If you want people to change, the first person you have to change is yourself.

Now is the time to pour into the people that spend more time with our kids then most parents.

If you're like most people, you have hopes and dreams of what you would like to accomplish in life.

For some people it's to impact the world; for other people it's creating their art, or having a life full of adventure and unpredictability.

If you chose to be an educator, don't let go of those dreams.

My hope is as you're reading you're inspired and provided with actionable steps to share your vision with your students and take action to create a life that shares your truth!

Unfortunately, too many people lose hope of what they desire in life or they never get started.

At some point in your life your energy was contagious and people couldn't get enough of you, and you had more than an abundance to share.

At some point in your life you have probably awakened suddenly to an especially vivid dream that inspired you. Those dreams are the coming attractions for your life.

Dreams are specific to you...Those dreams are your calling.

It's our responsibility to find our voice, follow our passion, and create a mission connected to our passion that will pull us forward through all of the doubt, criticism, pain, and fear.

Your mission will be the reason why you uncover your gift. Why isn't everyone living out their dreams?

Why isn't everyone creating a mission that's connected to their passion (more on this later in the book)?

When I ask people this question, the answer they often tell me... *life!*

"THERE'S ONLY ONE WAY TO GAIN GOOD JUDGMENT, THAT'S BY MAKING POOR DECISIONS. EXPERIENCE IS CREATED THROUGH BAD JUDGMENT." -TONY ROBBINS

EXPERIENCES ARE OUR GREATEST EDUCATOR

If you're looking to CREATE experiences in life, you'll have to do three things...

1) GET OUT OF YOUR COMFORT ZONE, physically, mentally, and emotionally.

Every memorable experience in my life as an athlete, a father, a husband, and entrepreneur, happened outside of the confines of my comfort level.

Get on the plane and get to that event. Sign up for a race six months before you're ready to run it. Buy that book you've been talking about reading today, and set a date for when you plan on completing it. Express your gratitude with a hand-written letter of thanks.

2) TAKE MASSIVE ACTION

Taking massive action has to take place when you're at an emotional peak. Nothing is going to be sustainable if you make decisions when your energy is low. Take massive action when your energy is HIGH, when you SEE the end before you've begun, and when going back is no longer an option.

3) GET A MENTOR

Who you surround yourself with is who you will become.

Mentorship isn't a new concept. Most people know they need a mentor but they don't know how to find one or who to seek mentorship through.

LET'S REFRAME MENTORSHIP:

- A mentor can be virtual. You don't need to be in their presence daily. You're going to have more than one mentor to guide you on how to fill each of the buckets of your life (more on choosing your life buckets in a later chapter).

- You don't need their permission for you to decide they're your mentor. Read and listen to their audiobooks, follow their content online, seek them out on Facebook, interact with them on LinkedIn, listen to their content through YouTube, and attend their live events. If you're consistent in how you interact with their content, they will eventually respond.

- When you have a chance to meet your mentor at an event, get on the plane, drive, take the train, get on the bus, do whatever it takes to be in their presence.

"GIVE YOUR CREATIVITY A VOICE"

Practice your craft every day. If you love to speak, create a video every day, go live on Facebook weekly, or join a speaking group. If you love working out, join an early morning training class, or hire a coach to train and push you. If it's music, write, sing, and record daily. Ten minutes is better than zero.

The reason why people give up on their dreams is that they stop practicing the thing they love, or they put a timeline on when they were supposed to have "made it."

You're going to make it if you get momentum, keep your momentum, and keep changing your approach until you get it.

Teaching is the beginning of your journey! Teaching is a beautiful way to express your passion to a captive audience and see what works and what doesn't.

Your classroom can become an incredible ecosystem that feeds your passion.

You have to identify and stay connected to your passion, and share it with your students as you teach. They will feel your authenticity and reciprocate by being more connected to you as a person, instead of being disconnected to your subject.

RECAP: CREATING A KARLDANNY EDUCATOR

A KarlDanny Educator knows…

…how to identify their gifts.

…that they need to get out of their comfort zone, take massive action, and get a mentor.

…that they need to have a mentor that has what they want in life.

…they need to get momentum, keep their momentum by doing something on a daily, and weekly basis (at a minimum) that's aligned with their gift.

"STOP COMPLAINING AND TAKE FULL RESPONSIBILITY FOR WHERE YOU ARE, YOU'RE THE REASON WHY YOU'RE IN THIS POSITION, YOU HAVE THE POWER TO GET YOURSELF OUT OF IT."

"TAKE IMPERFECT ACTION TODAY."
-SAM OVENS

3) OVERCOMING DOUBT

ALL ACHIEVERS HAVE DOUBT that creeps into their mind at some point! The difference between achievers and people that fall short of their desires is...

...Achievers know they're ready for the moment because the moment isn't about them. It's about the cause or people they believe in. DOUBT doesn't shake their confidence, faith, or prevent them from moving forward!

As an educator, have you noticed that you have incredible levels of confidence in the classroom, but are struggling with your health, your relationship, or with being happy?

In today's digital world, we typically see the highlight reels of people's lives.

But what we don't hear enough about are the stories of fear, pain, loss, doubt, and failure. Anyone you admire has a story to share.

Every time I've taken on a new endeavor, doubt has crept into my mind at some point. When doubt shows up because I'm teaching a new lesson, coaching a new group of athletes, or taking on a fitness challenge, I have trained my mind to tap into my momentum from the hours I have already put in to prepare.

Through preparation comes an intense level of confidence regardless of what you're preparing for: an observation, a new fitness routine, or posting a new endeavor online.

Achievers use their preparation and confidence from *other events* to fuel them as they're walking through a new endeavor.

"SOME PEOPLE SAY THEY HIT THE WALL... I'M TRAINING TO RUN THROUGH IT." -DAVID GOGGINS

At this point in my life, I'm proud to say I have spent time with—and studied—some of the highest achievers and performers in the world.

Here's a list of the most consistent practices and strategies achievers implement to help them achieve their ultimate prize.

As an educator, you can put these strategies into practice when you're outside the comfort zone of teaching inside your four walls.

VISUALIZE: Achievers see the finish line before they begin. They replay the finish over and over and over again on a continuous loop in their mind.

WHEN YOU DON'T KNOW WHERE TO START OR HOW YOU'LL FINISH: Achievers recognize they don't see all the steps necessary to achieve their goal, and they start anyway.

FEAR: Achievers are afraid to fail but aren't afraid of fear. Achievers are driven to avoid failure—they recognize that the only way to achieve is to overcome fear by believing in something bigger than themselves.

ACHIEVERS PRACTICE THE BASICS: The basics give achievers confidence. Achievers also recognize that the basics will never be boring and basic.

HABITS: Achievers have healthy habits that they practice daily. Achievers have training habits, nutritional habits, meditative habits, and connections to their church, faith, spirit, or the universe.

BEING ALONE: Achievers aren't afraid to be alone, but they recognize that they aren't going to achieve their goal by doing everything themselves.

FAILURE: Achievers celebrate their failures. They celebrate their failures by focusing on what they learned from the experience.

HUMBLE AMIABILITY: Achievers laugh at themselves when they're embarrassed. They see embarrassment as something funny to laugh about.

Achievers see embarrassment as an opportunity to share a funny story. When they reflect on the experience, they learn and grow from it, and achievers know embarrassment will only strengthen their resolve.

Achievers overcome doubt by smiling and laughing in the moment and not taking themselves too seriously.

RECAP: CREATING A KARLDANNY EDUCATOR

A KarlDanny Educator (Self-Aware - Empathetic - Curious) knows how to overcome doubt...

...by creating a vision for their life.

...by taking action even when they don't see all the steps necessary to cross the finish line.

...by moving forward in the face of fear.

...by practicing the basics.

...by having health daily habits—emotionally, physically and nutritionally.

...by being comfortable being alone.

...by knowing failure is part of the process but it doesn't define them.

...by laughing at themselves not taking everything too seriously.

"IT TAKES A GREAT (PERSON) TO GIVE SOUND ADVICE TACTFULLY, BUT A GREATER ONE TO ACCEPT IT GRACIOUSLY." -LOGAN PEARSALL SMITH

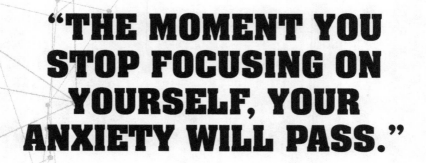

"THE MOMENT YOU STOP FOCUSING ON YOURSELF, YOUR ANXIETY WILL PASS."

4) FEELING ANXIOUS...NOW WHAT?

I WAS TAUGHT A LONG TIME AGO that the secret to living is giving.

When anxiety creeps in, it's typically because we're afraid to fail, we're in fear of judgment, or we're embarrassed.

But as quickly as the anxiety can show up, it can pass.

When you need to reduce anxiety, you need a change in your state! We can change our state instantly by changing what we focus on.

You can change what you focus on by creating a new emotion— emotion is created by motion.

One of the biggest issues of the pandemic was people were confined to their homes. People around the world were told to stay home.

People were home, watching the news (BLUES) and having their state alerted on a daily basis.

Our educators were asked to teach through a medium the majority haven't ever experienced and certainly weren't trained on.

During this time, America, as well as countries around the world, reported an overall increase in anxiety.

Here's the first step you can take to reduce your feelings of anxiety.

MOVE!

Use a power pose:

A study conducted at Columbia and Harvard concluded that standing in one of the suggested power poses—hands on your hips, or standing tall with your fingertips on a desk, for instance—for as little as a minute could decrease cortisol (the stress hormone).

Studies also found that you're 86% more likely to focus on rewards and benefits versus stress and feelings of overwhelm just from standing in a particular way.

"PUT ALL EXCUSES ASIDE AND REMEMBER THIS: YOU ARE CAPABLE" -ZIG ZIGLAR

Let's MOVE!

Get up, use a power posture stance! Go for a walk! Slow your breathing down! Take a few sips of water! Focus on taking deep, slow, controlled breaths.

If your anxiety is running rampant, stop focusing on yourself.

Stop focusing on what you aren't getting, how you've been treated unfairly, how it isn't your fault, how you're lonely, or how you failed.

You can immediately reduce your anxiety by focusing on how your current situation can create an opportunity to **give, create, or move on from.**

As educators, we have a tendency to hold on to things for too long, thinking one day we may need them. One day rarely comes…

If you're anxious over changing grades, moving classrooms, back to school night, an unannounced observation, or a pandemic, here's a list of phrases you can use to instantly change your state.

IF YOU WANT TO CREATE A NEW SKILL…

"By creating a new skill I will be able to share…"

IF YOU'RE FEELING ANXIOUS ABOUT MOVING ON FROM YOUR SCHOOL OR CHANGING LOCATIONS

"Moving out of the school, grade, or district will allow me to create a new…"

IF YOU'RE FEELING ANXIOUS ABOUT CREATING THAT BUSINESS YOU HAVE BEEN TALKING ABOUT…

"My new business will solve a major problem and help…"

IF YOU KNOW TRAVELING WILL HELP YOU CREATE A FRESH START BUT YOU HAVEN'T PLANNED THAT TRIP YET…

"I'm going to visit my friend/family in… It's been years and we will have a chance to reconnect."

IF YOU'VE RECENTLY LOST YOUR JOB AND NEED TO MOVE ON OR CHANGE PROFESSIONS…

"This is a great chance to write that book, start a VLOG, learn a musical instrument, or learn a new skill that will allow me do what I really want…"

Tell yourself the truth, but don't make it worse than it is.

IF YOU'VE STRUGGLED TO IMPROVE YOUR HEALTH AND CREATE A LIFE OF VITALITY AND ENERGY; IF YOU'RE FEELING HOPELESS THAT NOTHING IS EVER GOING TO WORK…

Ask yourself the following questions to get momentum:

"Losing weight is going to help me...?"

"Improving my health is going to make me feel...?

"How can I lose weight and enjoy the process?"

Ask yourself a *better a question*, and you'll be given a **better answer**.

These are the **wrong questions** to ask yourself...

"Why can't I lose weight?"

"Why do I always fail?"

"Why can't I be consistent?"

When you begin your health journey...

...be kind to yourself.

...let go of your past attempts.

...get a role model; no one does it alone.

IF YOU WANT TO MOVE ON FROM UNHEALTHY RELATIONSHIPS IN YOUR LIFE AND HAVE PEACE OF MIND...

Tell yourself a new story...

"___was really draining me. I forgot what it was like to be happy."

"I finally have a chance to focus on myself."

Changing your focus from what you aren't getting to what you have an opportunity to give, create, or remove will create a new sense of excitement and minimize your anxiety. (More on how to change your focus in the next chapter.)

Then you'll need to take immediate action towards what you want to GIVE and create.

TAKE ACTION IMMEDIATELY. Don't wait! Take action when your emotion is at its peak.

If you're taking action, you're doing something today that forces you to be committed to it tomorrow. If you took action and feel uncomfortable and nervous, you took the appropriate amount of action.

"DOUBT IS THE MIND'S WAY OF SAYING YOU NEED TO PREPARE. TAKE IMPERFECT ACTION!"

REMINDER... Emotion is created by motion; if you want to keep your positive energy high and your anxiety low, get yourself in motion towards your new opportunity.

Here are a few examples of how you can take action RIGHT NOW!

- Go for a walk.

- Make phone calls until the appointment is set.

- Sign up to workout with that CRAZY trainer.

- Book a trip and figure out the details when you get there.

- Sign up for that class RIGHT NOW.

Don't turn the page until you've taken action; that's how you're going to get momentum.

RECAP: CREATING A KARLDANNY EDUCATOR

- Emotion is created by motion, get up and move.

- If you want to reduce anxiety, stop focusing on yourself.

- Create a different language pattern if you're serious about reducing anxiety.

- Ask yourself better questions if you've fallen short of your goals in the past.

- Take massive action—do something that holds your feet to the fire tomorrow.

- Take imperfect action—figure everything else out along the way.

"STRENGTH DOES NOT COME FROM PHYSICAL CAPACITY. IT COMES FROM AN INDOMITABLE WILL." -MAHATMA GANDHI

"THE FEAR OF NOT BEING LOVED, AND THE POSSIBILITY OF NOT BEING ENOUGH, IS WHAT'S CAUSING YOUR ANXIETY."

5) ANXIETY IS HERE...NOW WHAT?

YOU'RE ENOUGH! Now repeat in first person: I'm enough! Repeat: I'm enough!! Repeat: I'm enough!!!

When anxiety creeps into the mind, achievers call it *stress*. An achiever would never call it what it really is...**FEAR!**

Fear of not being enough!

Fear of failing and not being loved!

The fear of losing the love you have if you fail!

That's what anxiety is at its core. That's what's causing you to feel paralyzed...Fear!

Change the story you're telling yourself when you feel anxious and you'll instantly change the way anxiety is impacting you.

This section is broken up into three parts. Implement one or all three parts and you will have the power you need to overcome anxiety.

I know everyone is experiencing an outrageous amount of anxiety during the pandemic.

As educators, we have to take care of ourselves first so we have something to give.

Repeat after me...

I'M READY TO OVERCOME MY ANXIETY!

Tell yourself the truth, but don't make worse than it is. The quicker you can get to the truth, the sooner you'll be able to overcome your fear.

"FEAR IS A HABIT, SO IS COURAGE."

When you get to the truth, you'll realize what you're fearing isn't as overwhelming as you originally thought. When you stay focused on who loves you—NO MATTER what the outcome—fear will still be present, but courage will pull you forward.

LOVE

Get clear on who loves you. Get clear on why they love you.

Why they love you has nothing to do with what you're feeling fearful of.

Their love for you isn't going to change if you don't achieve what you set out to accomplish.

Yes, they will celebrate you and be excited if you accomplish your goals. However, they aren't going to love you more, and they aren't going to love you less if you don't achieve your goals.

If you think their love for you will change, you haven't identified the right person that loves you...

...The people that love you and support the endeavor you're about to embark on.

Their love for you is eternal!

RE-read the above until it sinks into your spirit.

FOCUS

Whatever you focus on you're going to feel. Consider your focus similar to sonar. The mind is designed to keep you alive—it isn't designed to give you what you want.

When you focus on something you deem valuable, a part of your brain called the RAS (reticular activating system) is responsible for differentiating between what's important and what isn't important.

"REINFORCE IT...UNTIL IT BECOMES A HABIT."

For Example:

After you buy a new vehicle, you may notice that car or truck everywhere you drive. In reality, that car/truck has always been there... The mind didn't note it as important until you started to focus on what type of car you wanted to buy.

Consciously influencing your focus will help you improve your confidence and overcome your anxiety!

If you're an athlete, your focus can work the same way. If you're preparing for an observation, a job interview, or a new lesson, your focus should be on how:

- Well prepared you are.

- You're amongst a select number of people that have this opportunity— you've already won.

- You're choosing to be assessed; you aren't being forced to be assessed.

- You're going to be loved no matter what the result is;

However, if you focus on:

- Being exhausted while you're running... *you'll feel exhausted before you even start.*

- Your kids misbehaving... *your class will act out.*

- Not getting the job... *you won't get the job.*

- Having a conflict with your co-workers... *all you'll see and feel is conflict when your co-workers are speaking.*

"YOU HAVE A CHOICE IN HOW YOU RESPOND TO ANXIETY."

BEING BULLIED AT WORK

If you've ever been bullied at work or teach kids that have experienced being bullied, it's safe to say bullying causes an extreme sense of anxiety, specifically when they walk into the building each day.

Whatever you focus on you're going to feel.

From the moment you wake up, think about how much power you have, what you're proud of, and what you'll be proud of yourself for at the end of the day.

Stand tall; put your hands on your hips (power pose) until you feel like a tower of power.

The first step is that you have to participate in your own rescue.

You're on earth to make an impact—not to be bullied.

When you take the time to focus on building yourself up every day, you'll be more equipped to overcome the challenges the world presents to you in real time.

It doesn't mean you aren't going to have challenges. It doesn't mean the bully is going to instantly leave you alone. What it means is you'll be better equipped to tell yourself a different story when the bully—or difficult moment—shows up.

Over time those stories are going to lead to a different result.

If you focus on...

...being scared,

...feeling weak,

...not wanting to get hurt,

...what people are going to think about you,

...just wanting to be friends with the bully,

you're going to feel weak, you're going to look weak, and nothing is going to change.

WHO LOVES AND SUPPORT YOU?

Teachers don't typically mind working in groups, but they generally want to create their own classroom activities and work alone. As much as they help kids and families throughout the course of their career, they're usually awful about asking for help when they need it.

If you're being bullied, this is the time to lean on the people that love you and support you outside of the building.

The most challenging part of being bullied at work is that teachers typically connect their self-worth and value to the performance of their students, and how they're viewed by administrators, the families they work with, and their co-workers.

When an educator is being bullied at work it tears at the fabric of who they are as people.

Lean on the people that love you outside of the building. Tell them what you're going through, let them pour into your spirit— you may spend a whole school year without having that sense of reassurance when you're in the building.

That doesn't mean you can't form tighter bonds outside of work!

ASK YOURSELF BETTER QUESTIONS.

When anxiety creeps into the mind, start asking yourself the right questions. Odds are you're making less than empowering statements to yourself while at the same time you aren't asking good questions.

Ask yourself questions that empower you!

When you ask yourself poor questions, the mind provides you with poor responses!

For example:

You might ask yourself, "Why can't I keep this weight off?"

The mind may respond with, "Because you're lazy!"

The truth is, if you're taking the time to read this, the odds are you aren't lazy! You're most likely in the top 1% of people seeking a higher purpose in life.

So, instead of asking, "Why can't I keep this weight off?"...

...the question you should be asking is, "How can I lose weight and enjoy myself while I'm doing it?"

The mind will discover an answer that will pull you towards your goal, instead of pushing you towards it.

"PAIN IS PART OF THE PROCESS AND PROCEDURE. PAINKILLERS CAN'T LEAD US TO THE DESIRED RESULT."

When you're pulled towards your goal versus pushed, fatigue and fear won't prevent you from taking action!

When you're pushed, you'll fall prey to doubt, fatigue, fear, and pain.

Ask better questions and you'll change your life. When you change your questions, you'll achieve better results.

AFFIRMATIONS vs INCANTATION

When you're preparing to overcome doubt you'll need to create an incantation, not to be confused with an affirmation.

Affirmations are...

- What you visualize happening.

- Typically written down daily.

- Connected to having a positive mind or being a positive thinker.

Affirmations have their place and can be a helpful tool to practice.

However, when you want to overcome ANXIETY you'll need to create an INCANTATION.

"MOVE YOUR BODY WHEN YOU WANT TO CHANGE YOUR EMOTION."

An incantation is a phrase or routine you use to become the person you need to be when anxiety shows up...

For example:

Beyoncé becomes "Sasha Fierce" before she walks on stage. Sasha has no fear, no doubt—Sasha owns the stage.

Beyoncé is a mom, a wife, a sister, and a friend.

Beyoncé has a set of rituals, i.e. "incantations," she uses before she goes on stage that helps her become "Sasha Fierce." Because Sasha Fierce doesn't have anxiety.

Kobe Bryant "incanted" a mentality and a way of thinking to overcome doubt and all levels of anxiety:

The Kobe Bryant "MAMBA MENTALITY."

When you have the Mamba Mentality you wake up at 4 am, you're in the gym by 4:30 am and you love practicing the fundamentals.

When you have the Mamba Mentality you practice three times a day before 2 pm. 4:30 am-6:30 am, 8:30 am-10:30 am, 12:30 pm-2 pm.

When you have the Mamba Mentality you love being booed by the crowd.

When you have the Mamba Mentality you demand the ball at the end of the game with everything on the line.

Kobe was a #girldad, a husband, a coach, and a friend. The Mamba Mentality was an incantation Kobe used to help him win championships.

You'll need to create an incantation for yourself. The incantation needs to be specific to you and your needs.

Your incantation can be a phrase that you repeat and rituals you practice as you repeat your phrase.

An incantation helps you create the person you need to be to accomplish the challenge in front of you to be anxiety-free!

RECAP: CREATING A KARLDANNY EDUCATOR

- Focus on how you'll be loved no matter what.

- You can overcome the bully at work by pouring into the people that love you the most outside of the Building. Ask them for support and let them pour into your spirit.

- Change what you're focusing on, and you'll change how you're feeling.

- Emotion is created by being in motion. Get up and get moving.

- Ask yourself questions that empower you, not disempower you.

- Create an incantation that you feel in your spirit that gives you POWER before anxiety shows up.

"STOP FOCUSING ON YOURSELF WHEN YOU WANT TO OVERCOME FEAR."

"LIFE IS OURS
WHEN WE'RE BEING
CREATIVE."

6) YES, YOU CAN CREATE THE LIFE YOU WANT...EVEN IF YOU'RE STARTING LATER

I WANT YOU TO THINK BACK to when you were in 7th or 8th grade (13-14 years young). At some point, you had a realization about what you wanted to be.

If you didn't know what you wanted to be, odds are you were wildly passionate about something that gave you a huge sense of satisfaction.

You may have even appreciated or participated in a few of the activities below:

HUNTING AND FISHING

DRAWING

PHYSICALLY TRAINING

PLAYING SPORTS

TELLING JOKES

READING OR WRITING

CREATING MUSIC

MATH, SCIENCE, HISTORY

DANCING

BUILDING THINGS

ASKING QUESTIONS

COACHING OR TEACHING

COOKING

POSITIONS OF LEADERSHIP

Everyone has had something that they loved doing during their adolescent years. If you didn't have an opportunity to participate in what you loved doing, you may have dreamt about it or envisioned "IT" for yourself.

Then life happened!

"STEP BY STEP WE WILL GET YOU AHEAD. NOT NECESSARILY IN FAST SPURTS, BUT WE WILL PREPARE FOR THE FAST SPURTS." -CHARLIE MUNGER

At this point, you may have lost sight of your passion, forgotten who you are, or feel like you aren't growing. If we aren't growing we're dying. Life doesn't offer us plateaus.

You may have forgotten what your interests are or what hobbies stimulate you or what music you enjoy listening to.

7th and 8th grade is a time during adolescence when our passions come to the surface. Oftentimes, our gift will reveal our passion.

PLEASE REFER BACK to Chapter 1 for the definition of how to define your gift.

WHEN YOU TAKE THE TIME TO THINK ABOUT WHAT YOU LOVED DOING DURING ADOLESCENCE, OR DREAMT ABOUT DOING WHEN YOU WERE AN ADOLESCENT, IT'S IMPORTANT NOT TO THINK ABOUT WHAT JOB OR PROFESSION FITS YOUR INTERESTS. THE MOMENT YOU THINK, "I CAN'T DO THAT FOR A LIVING," YOU'RE THINKING TOO SMALL.

Your gift will make a way for you to discover and unlock your passion.

In today's world, having the ability to influence yourself and those around you to take action is your best asset. You can maximize your ability to influence by combining it with your passion. You can create the lifestyle and livelihood you desire by learning how to share your knowledge and your gift!

"WE'RE THE ONLY CREATURES ON EARTH THAT CAN CHANGE OUR EMOTIONS FROM FEAR TO JOY INSTANTLY."

Your gift doesn't have to fit into the conventional way of "earning a living." When you discover what your gift is, the key is to be aggressively patient when it comes to maximizing your passion.

STAY CONNECTED TO YOUR PASSION

If you love hair and makeup but feel as though teaching has lost its luster—or feel as though you have more to give but don't know where to start—share you passion for hair and makeup with the students in your school district.

Start a club! Offer a FREE six-week online course to the high school kids in your district. Meet once a week online and teach one aspect of makeup and hair each week.

Take that experience and videos of you teaching and share on your socials and with the local hair and makeup salons. Business owners will be intrigued to learn how you can add value to their salon and current clients with your online presence and approach.

Stay connected by consistently sharing your gift. Your GIFT (as stated in an earlier chapter) is the thing that you do best that requires the least amount of effort.

That doesn't mean it's going to be easy; it means you know what you have and that it's worth sharing!

"CHANGE YOUR FOCUS, CHANGE YOUR LIFE."

Do you know what stops most people—and definitely stops teachers—from getting started? It's not knowing the exact path to travel to achieve a desired outcome.

Educators are outcome driven—we have to be in our profession—but when you're sharing your gift you have to be MISSION driven!

If you want to feel like you're growing, create a mission and connect it to your gift.

Using the hair and makeup example above you can create a mission to empower high school students by helping them see their internal beauty through hair and makeup design.

Creating a mission connected to your gift will pull you through fear, rejection, and disappointment.

OVERCOMING REJECTION

Embrace rejection as one step closer to working with the right people—every time you hear NO!

Sharing your gift will give you the opportunity to face your fear of embarrassment...

We make embarrassment bigger than it really is. People will often tell me, it's the only thing people are going to say about me, it's the only thing people will remember.

The truth is, no one really cares once it's over. People move on! It doesn't matter who you are, what your social status is. People move on. They move on faster when you own it and move on from it yourself.

I can share countless examples of celebrities, athletes, and politicians that have embarrassed themselves.

Hasn't the world moved on from it? The world definitely moved on from it the moment they owned it.

Here are a few keys to help you keep momentum:

- Consistency is the KEY! Don't stop! Get a little smarter every day.

- Practice your craft every day. Share your craft every day.

- Create something that feeds your spirit: videos, journal entries, pictures, and/or books for instance. Creating something that becomes positively addicting to you is going to pique the interest of the people you want to impact.

BE PATIENT

You know what you want, but the world doesn't know you yet. It may take 6 months or 3 years to penetrate the marketplace.

Someone is going to eventually say yes and give you a shot!

When they look at your product, social network, or website, make sure they have every reason to move forward and hire you.

They should say, "It looks like they have been doing this for a while and know what they're doing."

HERE'S THE REASON WHY IT'S NEVER GOING TO BE TOO LATE:

The power of your WILL TO SUCCEED paired with the unprecedented access to the world of information and social connection through the internet.

Don't underestimate how much people didn't know before they got started.

You can hire a talented freelancer internet guru that can do anything for you…from designing a website, to creating sales copy, to logos, ads, etc.

Your first product (website or video) for the public won't look the same years from now… and you should be able to laugh at yourself years from now. Too many people don't ever get started because they're worried it isn't going to be perfect. Just get going!

SOLVE A PROBLEM

If you've been involved in an industry for more than 10,000 hours (about 5 years of hyper-focused work in one area) and have created consistent results, you're considered an expert in your field.

Now is the time to use your experience to your advantage.

If you have no experience in an industry, but see the problems that need to be solved, you might be at a greater advantage. You won't have preconceived notions of how things should be done, or how everyone else is doing it!

You might create a new pathway to achievement because you aren't following the traditional path.

Here are a few steps to help you get momentum towards your goal, regardless of what age you start:

STEP 1

Identify the problems within the industry you have experience in or want to disrupt. If you find yourself passionate about a cause and the people you want to serve, you're ready to go.

STEP 2

Apply your gift toward solving the problem.

- Take imperfect action and get started.

- Fall in love with who you want to serve, not the product or service. When you love who you're serving you'll be willing and ready to pivot based on their needs and desires.

- When you hear rejection, learn from it. You can change your path to achievement, but you don't have to change the destination.

That's right, don't quit because you have been at it for years and haven't broken through...the world is catching up to you.

"FAITH IS THE SUBSTANCE OF THINGS HOPED FOR, EVIDENCE OF THINGS NOT SEEN." -THE GOOD BOOK

Step 3

Build a team. Connect with a mastermind, Facebook group, freelancers, or any other group of people that are driven to be part of something bigger than themselves. Your team doesn't have to work directly with you. Even so, when you connect with them you should feel the momentum and a confirmation that you aren't always alone on this journey.

You have a story tell!

The empowering images in your mind and the inspiring dreams you're having at night are a preview of your life's coming attractions. A preview of the life you're meant to live!

RECAP: CREATING A KARLDANNY EDUCATOR

- Take imperfect action.

- Fall in love with your ideal customer, not your product or service. You'll be prepared to pivot based on their needs.

- Stay patiently connected to your passion, go for what you want.

Water the seed of your dream every day.

- Your dreams are the coming attractions of the life you're supposed to live if you go all in.

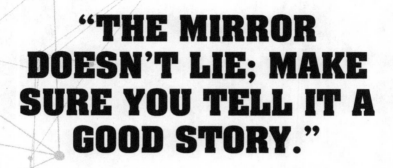

"THE MIRROR DOESN'T LIE; MAKE SURE YOU TELL IT A GOOD STORY."

7) CONFIDENCE IS CREATED; YOU AREN'T BORN WITH IT

SOMEONE TOLD YOU...*you're fat!*

Someone told you...*that you're too slow!*

Someone told you...*you're not an athlete!*

Someone told you...*you aren't an artist!*

Someone told you...*you can't build a business!*

Someone told you...*you will never leave this town!*

Someone told you...*you're broke, it isn't a good time!*

Someone told you...*you don't have a degree in that!*

Someone told you...*you're so ugly!*

Someone told you...*that looks terrible on you!*

If you're struggling to regain your confidence, it's because you believe what they said. And, because of your be-LIE-f, you've created a story to support their be-lie-fs.

The empowering thing is...rebuilding your confidence is your job!

And nobody can take it away once you do the work for yourself.

HOW TO REBUILD YOUR CONFIDENCE

Connect with someone that believes in you! Hopefully, the first people that believed in you are your parents. If so, connect with them, and let them know that you aren't satisfied.

Odds are they won't have the answers you need, but hearing a positive response from someone that supports you will help you grasp the most impactful aspect of achievement...MOMENTUM!

"YOU'RE NOT A VICTIM. YOU'RE A VICTOR." -ERIC THOMAS

Regardless of the relationship you have (or don't have) with your parents, it's important to understand that you need to have a daily routine that rebuilds your confidence.

There have been plenty of people that have achieved without the support of their parents. You might be one of them. But remember, no one has done it alone!

It's your responsibility to connect with that person that has an unwavering layer of support for you. Everyone has someone that believes in them.

HOW TO GET MOMENTUM

Reframe what you envision as a WIN.

"EVERYTHING CAN BE TAKEN FROM A MAN BUT ONE THING; THE LAST OF THE HUMAN FREEDOMS—TO CHOOSE ONE'S ATTITUDE IN ANY GIVEN SET OF CIRCUMSTANCES, TO CHOOSE ONE'S OWN WAY." -VIKTOR FRANKL, SURVIVOR OF NAZI CONCENTRATION CAMP, AUTHOR

Wins can be as simple as:

- Making your bed every morning.

- Drinking 32 oz of water as soon as you wake up.

- Meditating daily for 5-15 minutes.

- Choosing an app, finding a studio, or starting a yoga routine to incorporate deep breathing into your daily habits.

Learning how to control your breathing will help you stay centered, calm, and creative. While you're breathing, focus on taking the breath from your lower abdomen. 5-15 minutes daily should be spent on deep diaphragm breathing. (More to follow in our chapter on nutrition.)

Get into a routine! Breath is life. It's the body's way of cleansing itself from disease, stress, and pain.

The trick is to feed the mind early in the day with a sense of accomplishment before the world starts demanding your attention.

WAYS TO BOOST WINS AND GET MOMENTUM

- Read a book about someone that has had a harder life than you. Contrast is a powerful way to feel as though you have momentum and a great way to build your confidence. Seeing how hard someone else's life is will make you feel better about yours.

- Say thank you to someone that has helped you or provided you with powerful and helpful insight into life.

- Practice your religious beliefs. I'm a Christian by faith and enjoy attending a bible-based church. Whatever your religious or spiritual practice is, PRACTICE it. You won't create a sense of confidence without acknowledging what you have and what you're appreciative of.

"HOW ARE YOU GOING TO MAKE SOMEONE ELSE BETTER? GOD WILL BLESS YOU AS HE TRUSTS YOU...AS YOU GROW, HOW ARE YOU GOING TO SHOW SOMEONE ELSE HOW TO MAKE IT?"

- GIVING is the secret to living. Write someone a note of gratitude. Buy a cup of tea for the stranger in line behind you. Pick up the phone and call a friend to say hello. Let them know, "I was just thinking about you." Doing things like this will make someone's day a little brighter, and you will feel amazing for doing it.

- Creating confidence is about creating triggers in your spirit that help you overcome doubt when doubt shows up (see Affirmations vs Incantations). When doubt shows up, have an incantation in your spirit that can help you instantly change your perspective.

- MOVE! Emotion is created by Energy in Motion (E-Motion)... If you're lacking confidence right now, odds are you're focusing on yourself. You're probably even sitting or lying down while you're doing it. You can instantly change the serotonin levels in your body by moving aerobically. 40-60 minutes of aerobic exercise (exercising in a way that allows you to still hold a conversation) will change your state and give you a sense of accomplishment and confidence.

RECAP: CREATING A KARLDANNY EDUCATOR

- Get a win first thing in the morning before the world starts demanding your attention.

- If you lack confidence, it's because you believe what people have said to you and about you.

- You have the power to influence your mind and stay focused on what you want.

- The secret to living is giving; make someone else's day better and you'll be rewarded by feeling great about yourself.

- Emotion is created by motion; get up and get moving! Joy and pain can't reside in the same place. E-MOTION will give you an opportunity to feel great.

"THE CHAINS OF HABIT ARE TOO WEAK TO BE FELT UNTIL THEY ARE TOO STRONG TO BE BROKEN."

8) IT'S MY BODY; NOW IT'S TIME TO RECLAIM IT

THE BODY IS THE VEHICLE of the spirit. It's amazing what it can do when treated with respect, good fuel, and the movement it needs to operate at its fullest. It gets even more amazing when we connect the body back to the earth on a daily basis by taking off our shoes and connecting our bare feet to the ground.

That's part of my personal spiritual perspective on health.

If you eat well, exercise, and learn how to enjoy yourself in the process, you're going to love how you look, you're going to love how you feel, and you're going to love how much more confidence you have.

That's my emotional-physical perspective on health.

THE CHALLENGE: EMOTIONAL EATING

You're an emotional eater if...

- You're eating in the middle of the night (or any time of day for that matter) to overcome stress and anxiety.

- You're constantly waiting for everyone to leave before you eat so you can eat alone.

- You eat when you're bored.

- You're eating to avoid social interactions.

"WHAT YOU FOCUS ON YOU'RE GOING TO FEEL." -TONY ROBBINS

I'M READY FOR A CHANGE, PLEASE SHOW ME HOW

First, you aren't the problem! It isn't your fault that food has become a source of comfort for you. At your core, what you're really looking for when you emotionally eat is a sense of peace. Fortunately, you found a way to achieve the peace you're seeking. Unfortunately, you've found peace in addicting foods that typically cause people to overeat.

STOP putting yourself down for eating to feel good! You haven't learned the skills to replace your emotional connection to food. Would you think someone's a failure if they never learned how to ride a bike or swim? Odds are you would say, "It isn't your fault. No one taught you." Managing your emotional connection to food is a skill that can be taught.

HOW TO ACHIEVE

1) First, we have to identify when you're eating. Late-night? After an argument with your parents? After an argument with your significant other? When you're stressed out about work or your kids' performance? When you're feeling hopeless? While watching movies or scrolling through your phone?

2) We have to practice good habits to change our state. Food causes a state change! All of the blood rushes to your stomach after you eat, your breathing slows down, and you feel in control. See Chapter 3 for how to manage your focus.

3) We have to replace eating with something that can bring you comfort.

    a) Change what you're focusing on.

    b) Practice 5 minutes of deep diathermic breaths.

    c) Drink warm green tea, something soothing.

    d) Choose to eat a serving size of almonds, have a bowl of Nice Cream portioned and prepared to eat, (more on that in our nutrition section).

    e) Have a meal replacement shake ready.

    f) Slow down when you eat! Give your body a chance to feel satisfied. If you allow your body to catch up to the mind you'll start to feel full.

    g) THROW OUT all of the sugar and no sugar added snacks in the pantry and celebrate while you're doing it.

"EMOTION IS CREATED BY MOTION. SO, GET UP AND MOVE! YOU'LL CREATE A NEW EMOTIONAL REALITY."

THE CHALLENGE: I HAVE BEEN LIKE THIS MY WHOLE LIFE.

I'm too skinny!

I'm too heavy!

I'M READY FOR A CHANGE, PLEASE SHOW ME HOW

First of all, be patient! STOP comparing yourself to other people. You're never going to have (the love) the body you want until you respect and appreciate the ability and beauty you currently possess.

I'm too heavy!

Here's a simple equation we're going to follow moving forward: burn more calories than you eat daily. That's it!

We have to bring weight loss into perspective. The media has made weight loss appear complicated. People become overwhelmed and don't ever get started, or they end up following a program that isn't sustainable to their lifestyle and beliefs.

Weight loss has to be seen as something simple, or we won't ever follow it.

"YOU CAN'T CONTROL THE EVENT, YOU CAN'T CONTROL THE OUTCOME, YOU CAN ONLY CONTROL YOUR RESPONSE."

THE CHALLENGE: CHOOSING THE RIGHT THING TO EAT IS SO CONFUSING, WHERE DO I START?

You're not alone. There are countless aisles and shelves in every supermarket you visit that are packed with the kinds of food that should never be sold to people wanting to be healthy.

GOAL...create a menu that fits your lifestyle that's measurable and repeatable.

Measurable: estimated number of calories consumed daily. Repeatable: estimated number of calories burned daily.

When you have your menu and your exercise routine, just get moving! Forget perfection!! JUST START MOVING!

I'M READY FOR A CHANGE, PLEASE SHOW ME HOW

You NEED a mentor. You're right, it is confusing. The food industry wants to keep you confused. If you're confused you'll make an impulsive choice when you're out—typically an unhealthy choice.

You need access to a mentor. Someone that you can ask questions specific to you and your goals. The most efficient way to create lasting change with a nutrition program is to work with someone that makes eating simple! Eating isn't complex, and eating food that helps you look and feel good shouldn't be complicated either.

HOW TO ACHIEVE

1) Your mentor should be someone that has a proven track record of working with someone your age and weight and has helped people achieve the same goals you have.

Eating like an IG model isn't going to get you their body. You need a customized program.

2) How To Find a Mentor

...ASK!

You need access to a mentor. Someone to whom you can pose questions specific to you and your goals. The most efficient way to create lasting change with a nutrition program is to work with someone that makes eating simple! Eating isn't complex! Online resources are great, but they're just resources.

Nothing can replace human interaction, so start by asking someone that has the body you want. If they have maintained their health for 5-10 years they aren't lucky. They're doing something you aren't doing. Ask them what they do, who they're working with, or who they recommend that you can speak to—send that person a text message, DM, hand-written letter, or call them.

In my experience folks in the health profession are happy to help get you going with a free consultation. Send them a message, ask for 30 minutes of their time. If they say no, odds are you wouldn't want to pay them for their knowledge. If they say no, find someone else.

3) If you can afford to see a functional medical doctor, GO ALL IN! Functional medicine and functional medicine doctors are the future of medicine! Functional medicine will be the reason why

the medical industry and medical schools change how traditional medicine is practiced and studied around the world.

4) The right person will teach you the four most important aspects of nutrition:

A - DEEP DIAPHRAGM BREATHING. Breathing in for 1 second, holding it 4, breathing out for 2 seconds.

B - PROPER HYDRATION. Drinking ½ your body weight in ounces of water daily.

C - AEROBIC FITNESS. Training in a way that allows you to carry on a conversation 35-45 minutes, minimum 5 days a week.

D - MICRO AND MACRO-NUTRIENTS, YOUR MICROBIOME, AND WHOLE FOODS.

These are the non-negotiables of nutrition. When traditional medicine and nutrition fail to teach people these foundations of nutrition, we're misleading our society into thinking that nutrition is solely based on healthy eating and self-control. In fact, as you can see, the foundation of healthy nutritional habits doesn't begin with food at all.

THE CHALLENGE: I NEVER FOLLOW THROUGH; I START WELL, BUT DON'T EVER FINISH.

This is a common issue and it has everything to do with gaining momentum and the commitment you have toward achieving your goal.

"YOU HAVE A CHOICE ON HOW YOU WOULD LIKE TO RESPOND."

I'M READY FOR A CHANGE, PLEASE SHOW ME HOW

The most powerful force in the human spirit is our need to stay consistent with how we define ourselves. The reason why you aren't following through is that it will force you to redefine WHO you are.

Are you carrying extra weight? Do you self-destruct a positive relationship, or self-sabotage an opportunity to work with someone that can help you? You've followed the same pattern for so long it's familiar and safe to you.

Now is the time to bet on yourself. Finishing is going to empower you to become more of the person you really are.

The truth is, you know you have more to share, more to give, and want to experience more! Your current weight is predictable, it's safe. You aren't holding back because you're shy, or don't have the time to train. You're afraid that the person you really want to be won't be enough!

HOW TO ACHIEVE

1) Start by telling yourself the truth, but don't make it worse than it is.

2) When you're ready to finally follow through and become a finisher, give yourself a due date and announce it publicly!

YES! That's right. Publicly.

If the thought of that sounds terrifying (PERFECT), pressure makes DIAMONDS for a reason. Your fear is the mind talking to you. The truth is never as scary as the stories the mind creates. Don't make it bigger than it is.

3) If you're in a relationship you're really passionate about and both of you have agreed that you feel committed to each other, come clean and tell her/him that you've made commitments to change your body in the past and have fallen short of your goals.

Step 3 is a critically important step...

"TEAMWORK MAKES THE DREAM WORK."
-JOHN MAXWELL

If you're in a relationship, you'll need their support to change your body. They have to be on board. Eating out, late-night movie snacks, or having a lethargic approach to aerobic training isn't going to help you. IN FACT...You may hit your goals, but you won't maintain the results. Your partner has to become your biggest fan and part of your accountability team.

If you're with the right person, they will protect you against your own vulnerabilities. They will put you in a position to achieve your goals. If they aren't helping you, they're hurting you. There are no plateaus in fitness. You're either getting better or you're getting worse.

RECAP: CREATING A KARLDANNY EDUCATOR

- Get a mentor if you're serious about improving your health—someone who has the body you want, and has been able to maintain it. Follow their pattern.

- Mentors are typically happy to offer a free consultation to get you started so you can get momentum (hopefully that provides you with enough reasons to stop saying why you can't take action now).

- The reality is, something is allowing you to remain comfortable with your health—please don't let fear hold you back! You're worth it.

- Review the foundational principles of health outlined above.

- You need the people closest to you to become your support system—no one does it alone.

"DON'T FOLLOW YOUR PASSION...DEFINE YOUR MISSION. WHEN YOU DEFINE YOUR MISSION IT WILL FUEL YOUR PASSION."

9) THE SECRET IS TO CREATE A MISSION, NOT TO JUST FOLLOW YOUR PASSION

HAVE YOU EVER BEEN TOLD to just follow your passion and everything will work out? Maybe your passion is still teaching, maybe it isn't.

Regardless of where you're at emotionally in your teaching career, having a mission is going to provide you with a sense of clarity and excitement to start the day with a fresh perspective.

Reflecting back on my high school days, my passion was sports, training, friends, youth coaching, and hanging out!

I remember when our high school hosted a career fair. To their credit, I thought it was well done and organized. Different experts from various fields of business held seminars and shared the various verticals of their fields.

I remember walking away thinking...I just want to make an impact!

But I don't know how to do that by following my current passion.

Then I read a phrase that changed my life...

TAKE IMPERFECT ACTION!

That's the key to unlocking the secrets of your life. At some point you're going to be given a sneak peek into the life you're meant to live.

Maybe you're living your dream right now. If you're not, I would like to dare you to daydream and remember a time when you felt so excited about the future the days flew by.

Your sneak peek may come in the form of a dream or a vision—but you're going to be given an opportunity to see the life you're meant for.

The question is, what are you going to do about it?

I mentioned in an earlier chapter that achievers don't see all of the details and obstacles before they begin their journey.

...They just start.

"MAKE REST A NECESSITY...NOT THE OBJECTIVE." -JIM ROHN

The challenge is, some people think they need a full understanding of an industry before they step into it or need experience writing grants or proposals for their classroom.

The most important thing is to start chasing your vision. Regardless of what you know or don't know, your passion will open new opportunities for you to manifest what you envision for your life.

Now that you're ready to TAKE IMPERFECT ACTION...

...LET'S CREATE YOUR MISSION.

Your mission is different from your passion. Your passion might be teaching music…

Your mission can be to bring joy to children by sharing beautiful music.

Your passion might be cooking or baking…

Your mission can be to reduce food waste and redistribute food to the needy.

Your passion might be math…

Your mission might be to bring financial literacy to high school students in your town/state or country.

Your passion might be working out...

Your mission might be to empower people around the world to improve their mental health through fitness.

Your passion might be to make a lot of money…

Your mission might be to create new life experiences for your family and friends that they couldn't create for themselves.

When you're clear on what your mission is, you'll be able to create a pathway of achievement to accomplish it.

"DON'T ASK FOR IT TO BE EASIER, ASK TO BE STRONGER."

STAY CONNECTED TO THE MISSION.

Your mission will lead you towards a life of fulfillment, contribution and achievement.

If your passion doesn't allow you to fulfill your mission, you'll have feelings of dissatisfaction, frustration, and disappointment—regardless of how much you're achieving.

"SUCCESS WITHOUT FULFILLMENT IS THE ULTIMATE FAILURE." -TONY ROBBINS

Your mission will lead you towards a life of fulfillment and contribution.

When you're in a position to fulfill your mission through your passion, you've arrived!

Creating a mission for your life will refuel your passion for education. You'll start to see new opportunities within the profession that will allow you to grow and fulfill your mission.

If you're preparing to graduate and haven't secured your first teaching position, I hope the next section provides you with a great perspective and momentum to secure your dream position.

NO-QUIT MENTALITY OF CAREER SEEKERS

Here's something that will make you think: There aren't enough people saying, "work at a job you aren't passionate about."

If that job allows you get momentum towards your mission, do it!

It's temporary, as long as you're taking steps towards your mission.

Here are some examples of success. I have paraphrased their missions and summarized their job histories.

Sara Blakely (Founder of Spanx)

Mission: to create a product that inspired women.

Job: she sold fax machines while she was working on creating a career to fulfill her mission.

Daymond John (Founder of FUBU)

Mission: To create a global fashion brand.

Job: He worked at Red Lobster while he was working on building a fashion empire.

Tony Robbins (Life and Professional Development Strategist)
Mission: To end suffering in people.

Job: Worked as a night custodian, which allowed him to learn and practice his craft during the day.

When you define and identify your mission, working a job you aren't passionate about will give you a stronger perspective on why you need to stay committed to your mission. The moment you walk into the opportunity you were destined to live, you'll realize you have a chance to live out life's purpose for your life.

I want to take a moment to reinforce this….

DON'T SPEND THE NEXT 30 YEARS DOING THINGS YOU AREN'T PASSIONATE ABOUT.

Define your mission and do whatever you have to do on a daily basis to build momentum to accomplish it.

Creating a mission for your life will fuel your passion and allow you to feel fulfilled as you pursue a career.

Progress = Happiness

"BEING HUMBLE AND STAYING PATIENT WILL ALLOW YOU TO BECOME THE PERSON YOU'RE MEANT TO BE."

RECAP...THIS IS SO IMPORTANT I BELIEVE IT'S WORTH REPEATING:

We have amazing leaders and educators in our school system. But the traditional ways of learning and sharing information through our educational system are broken.

After four years of high school and college, the odds of you knowing what you want to do for the rest of your life (that's fulfilling and meaningful) are, at best, unlikely.

Being clear on your mission will act as the north star when you graduate, and as you navigate life through your teaching career.

"ACHIEVEMENT IS SOMETHING YOU ATTRACT, NOT SOMETHING YOU PURSUE." -JIM ROHN

Creating a mission that evolves as you evolve will free you from feeling bad about yourself, if you don't have a job before you graduate or within a year of two out of college.

If you're working in a profession that allows you to fulfill your mission, the years of experience you'll gain by being in the workforce, and the joy you'll be creating by fulfilling your mission, will be time well spent!

HOW TO DEFINE YOUR MISSION

See Chapter 1 on identifying your gifts. When you share your gift with the world, you've effectively defined your mission.

HOW TO PUT YOUR MISSION INTO ACTION

1) GET MOMENTUM. Do one thing a day to make yourself a little more knowledgeable than yesterday.

2) DON'T OVERTHINK IT! Don't worry about how to change the world in a week. Just be clear on what problem you want to solve, and who you want to serve.

3) SHARE YOUR SHORT TERM GOALS on socials but don't share your mission. The "goal" of sharing your short term goals on socials is to apply social pressure to yourself. When you have pressure to move forward, the most common tendency of people is to move forward. When the majority of people feel comfortable with the process, they ease up and become complacent.

4) THE MISSION YOU HAVE FOR YOUR LIFE IS YOURS—don't share it with people. The majority of people will shoot it down because they won't understand it. The only people you should share your mission with are people that you believe can help you achieve it.

5) When you're on a mission, **YOU'LL NEED TO SAY NO**...NO to hanging out every weekend. NO to buying an expensive car. NO to living in an amazing apartment or house a few months or years out of school. Accomplishing your mission is worth the delays in immediate gratification. Spend four to five years (at a minimum) saying NO and you'll be so much closer achieving your dreams.

6) SEEK MENTORSHIP! Someone with more experience that has the level of impact you aspire to create. Connect with that person on socials, listen to their YouTube videos and podcasts, read their books, and instill their habits into your life.

ACHIEVEMENT LEAVES CLUES. Follow their lead, learn from their mistakes, and you'll save time, money, aggravation, and maximize your impact.

RECAP: CREATING A KARLDANNY EDUCATOR

- Define your gift.

- Take imperfect action.

- Apply your gift to help you create a mission that's bigger than getting a teaching job and securing tenure.

- Achievement leaves clues. Learn from the mistakes, but they don't have to be yours—get a mentor that has the impact you desire. Yes, having a mentor teacher is great. Having a mentor that has had the impact you desire is the key to growing when you're a veteran teacher.

- Mentors can be found by reading books, watching videos, and creating daily habits that fuel your mission.

"LEADERS ANTICIPATE. LOSERS REACT." -TONY ROBBINS

10) WHY AN ATHLETIC MINDSET WILL HELP YOU ACHIEVE EVERYTHING YOU WANT

IF YOU NEVER PLAYED A HIGH SCHOOL OR COLLEGE SPORT, this chapter may read like a foreign object to you.

If you played a sport or have a passion for sports, please pay attention.

I'm going to outline how championship teams are formed, how effective leaders cultivate a team, and why you need an 'us-against-the-world-for-a-cause' mentality to win. Applying each of these principles to your life after sports will be the reason why you achieve and inspire people beyond your wildest dreams.

GRIT

Grit is a reality our educational leaders have recognized as a necessity our students need to achieve in the world we live in. Grit is having the ability to be resilient through challenging moments and situations.

Here's the truth!!!

If you don't want to hear the truth skip this section on GRIT. If you aren't practicing it, hopefully this serves as a wake-up call.

Everyone reading this has GRIT...

Everyone has something that you would push through no matter what the obstacle is. Maybe it's for your kids, a cause you're passionate about, or your business.

The reality is...

...the majority of the population has become so soft they don't even know how to teach grit because they aren't practicing it!

We need students to have GRIT during exams, writing lessons, research projects, and various challenges in school.

How can we expect students to possess something the adults they're interacting with on a daily basis don't practice themselves?

If you aren't challenging your GRIT on a daily to weekly basis, you aren't qualified to teach someone how to implement it into their lives.

GRIT doesn't show up because you tell someone that they need to have it.

GRIT is a seed that you plant in the mind. The only way to water it is through daily (at a minimum weekly) physical and/or mental exercises that make you uncomfortable!

That's IT!

We're living in a world where people don't want to make themselves uncomfortable. We don't want to let our kids get uncomfortable.

- Is your body a representation of the GRIT that's in your heart?

- Is your relationship a representation of the GRIT that's in your spirit?

- Is your career a representation of how much GRIT you have to share with the world?

If you answered no to any of those questions, I'm wildly confident that you have an area of your life that does represent your GRIT.

Perhaps you show your grit by stretching yourself to consistently provide your kids with opportunities.

Perhaps you show your grit by always being prepared when you walk into your classroom.

Perhaps it's been so long that you've forgotten what it's like to challenge the GRIT that's in your heart.

If we want students to have more GRIT while they're taking on their school academics, hire someone that consistently demonstrates GRIT that can share their perspective.

Again, if you want students to have more GRIT, they need to water that seed in the mind with physical and/or mental challenges daily, or at a minimum weekly.

If we want our students to have more GRIT, we need our educational leadership and educators to water the seed of their own mind—with physical and/or mental challenges. You're the person our kids want to relate to the most!

GRIT can only be taught if you embody it yourself.

HOW CHAMPIONSHIP TEAMS ARE FORMED

One thing has to change when you're preparing to do something you've never done or to return to a level of dominance that helped your program create a name for itself.

RAISE — THE — STANDARD

It may seem elementary, or too simple. But simple doesn't

necessarily mean easy. The way that you raise the standard in an athletic program is to bring in a new coaching staff or coach the existing staff up with personal development programs. This will teach and encourage them to raise the standards in their personal life giving them the opportunity to raise the standards of the athletes and staff they lead.

"AN AUTHENTIC APOLOGY IS A CHANGE IN BEHAVIOR." -UNKNOWN

An uninspired leader can't inspire the people around them. A leader that doesn't challenge themselves will never know how much his players are capable of being challenged.

In education the same rules apply…

Raising the standard begins with the leader raising it for themselves first!

Give More

Give more of your personal time to the staff. Get out of your office, specifically on the secondary level.

Give more to the kids in the building. Share a meal with students. Attend their athletic events and become their biggest cheerleaders.

Love More

As a leader, if you want to bring out the best in your staff, you'll need to love them more. Learn the goals, desires, and aspirations for every member on your staff. Help them get there. If you want your teachers to perform at a higher level, help them achieve their dreams. They will be all in everyday!

Connecting On A Deeper Level

As a leader, you need to learn how to connect more deeply to the needs of your students and staff. The greatest leaders understand how to apply the four most essential needs we share as people.

CERTAINTY - UNCERTAINTY - LOVE/CONNECTION - SIGNIFICANCE

When you understand how to fulfill the needs of your staff as people, you will unlock the greatness of everyone in your building.

Showing Up

Leaders have to be consistent. Leaders have to be a pillar of strength and calm. They have to show up with a great attitude, as well as the ability to tell the truth without making it worse than it is. Leaders lead with empathy.

HOW TO TRANSFER A CHAMPIONSHIP TEAM'S MENTALITY TO YOUR LIFE AFTER SPORTS

You need to put yourself around people that are playing the game of life and business at another level. You'll never know what you're really capable of accomplishing until you see people accomplishing things you've never imagined.

Roger Bannister set out to run a 4-minute mile at a time when it was an athletic accomplishment that had never been done in sports.

People told him it was impossible, that he would die trying because his heart wouldn't be able to take the pressure.

After he broke the 4-minute mile barrier, his record was broken 46 days later. Before Bannister, a 4-minute mile was seen as impossible. Since that time more than 1000 people have broken the 4-minute mile barrier—including high school kids.

What Changed? Roger Bannister...

RAISED — THE — STANDARD

When I walked into the team meeting of my first high school varsity lacrosse position, I told everyone in the room that we will be a championship program and we will win a state championship.

I said that everything we do moving forward will be in preparation of becoming a champion.

How did we win nearly 50 games in 4 years? Why was I selected as a High School Lacrosse Coach of the year after 3 years? How did we become a championship program?

We raised the standard!

Here are a few examples of how you can raise the standard in your life...

- Join a mastermind that has an eclectic group of achievers or an entrepreneur group that can provide a different perspective on the world. Teachers have a tendency to only hang out with other teachers. A new group will create a new perspective, new insight, and create new opportunities to be more creative.

- Work with a mentor, coach, or accountability partner to improve an aspect of your life unrelated to teaching. You'll carry the momentum to every other aspect of your life. Make sure it's someone that has the lifestyle and experiences you desire.

- Hire a personal trainer. Train with a workout partner—a coach that challenges you to push beyond your threshold of control. If you aren't prioritizing your health, you won't be able to enjoy the fruits of your labor.

"YOUR FEAR OF LOOKING STUPID IS WHAT'S HOLDING YOU BACK." -UNKNOWN

HOW EFFECTIVE LEADERS CULTIVATE A TEAM AND BUILD A STAFF THAT WON'T WANT TO DISAPPOINT YOU!

I have always defined discipline as creating expectations, not obligations.

One of the first steps effective leaders take when they enter into a new year or position is to instill discipline into their program.

Often when people initially hear the word discipline, they connect it to giving something up, taking something away, being yelled and screamed at for not following directions, or being led by a dictator.

Those are examples of ways to instill discipline, but they aren't examples of effective leadership.

DISCIPLINE:

Team leaders and assistant principals should have an *on–time is late, early is on time* mentality. The leaders on your team can never be late. Leaders have to hold the members of their team accountable if they aren't on time.

LESSON TO APPLY:

Hold yourself accountable as a school leader. If the leader isn't going to be on time for a meeting, it needs to be communicated before the meeting is scheduled to begin. Not when you arrive. Too often, school leadership demonstrates a *the meeting starts when I get there* mentality. It shows a complete lack of respect to the staff and community members we serve.

If you aren't going to hold yourself to the highest standard, you don't have the right to pressure your staff to show up on time. If you pressure your staff but don't practice it yourself or communicate when you're going to be late, you'll never get their best effort or respect.

DISCIPLINE:

When the floor is level and the rules are clear for everyone, leaders need to remove or change the positions of members from the school that don't put the needs of the building first. Regardless of their talent or lack of talent, they're either adding to the school or subtracting... no exceptions. If they aren't adding, their position and influence has to change.

LESSON TO APPLY:

Remove members of the staff that don't complement the team! In school, the squeaky wheel gets what it wants. Good people that do their job are often inconvenienced to satiate the loudest and most miserable people in the building.

It needs to stop.

Remove the person that doesn't fit with the team from their position. I'm not calling for the person to be fired. I am calling for leadership to take care of the people that are doing everything they're supposed to do. Work with union leadership in your district and take care of the quiet soldiers that make your building run.

"LEARN TO WORK HARDER ON YOURSELF THEN YOUR JOB." -JIM ROHN

DISCIPLINE:

Schedule time for the staff to eat together. Good teams and great staffs have meals together.

LESSON TO APPLY:

The highest performing staffs have scheduled meals together throughout the entire school year.

Eating together during lunch is easier to apply in the primary grades but is more challenging on the secondary level due to scheduling conflicts.

The grade-level leadership should be taught to have "impromptu" lunches or dinners throughout the year—a Thursday smoothie bar run as a grade-level, or a summer party off school grounds. The point is, a staff that eats together stays together.

A competitive game of cards, or a fun badminton match are creative ways to instill a sense of community and unity in the building.

School should be fun!

Cultivating competitive and celebratory opportunities into your buildings will create emotional connections between the teachers and support staff. When emotion is sparked, memories become unforgettable.

As the leader of your building, encourage your team leaders to connect with their departments during the holidays. If a leader would like to cultivate a family atmosphere, they need to follow the same routines families traditionally follow during the holidays.

These steps shouldn't be confused with how you create culture. Culture is created by how you, as the leader, consistently show up to meet the needs of your people.

DISCIPLINE:

Elite teams have matching Swag. Teachers should follow the same pattern.

LESSON TO APPLY:

Create swag that doesn't represent your union leadership—typically worn on a Friday. School swag is what leadership creates that speaks to who you are as a building. It brings everyone together.

"THE UNIVERSE WILL MAKE WAY FOR YOUR DREAMS WHEN YOU BECOME INTENTIONAL."

DISCIPLINE:

Show up every day dressed for the job you want, not for the job you have.

LESSON TO APPLY:

As the school leader, show up every day dressed and prepared to represent the building and community you're part of. When you're on field trips or attending a weekend event, relax—everyone knows you're still in charge. It's a great time to be more relatable and connect with your students and staff.

DISCIPLINE:

Being consistent is a form of discipline. Doing the work, showing up, and doing the things you said you're going to do will put you amongst the elite as a leader.

LESSON TO APPLY:

Hire for your weaknesses, not for your strengths. Bring in people that close the loop on your blind spots. It will make you more effective, timely, and respected by your staff. It will actually make them love you, because you'll become someone that they can count on.

You'll become a pillar of strength, not an incompetent BOSS.

"REGRET HURTS MORE THAN FAILURE."
-KVNDM

DISCIPLINE:

Surround yourself with like-minded people from various fields of leadership. Who you surround yourself with is who you will become!

LESSON TO APPLY:

Covid-19 has brought out a level of stress and anxiety in our leadership unlike any time in our educational history.

Connect your mind on a daily basis to who you want to become in your life.

If your mind is only connecting with the negativity at work, the demands of the community, or the board of education, you'll never harness your personal power.

You need to create a standard of connecting with leaders outside of education that offer a refreshing perspective on life and work, and have the ability to share a perspective far more difficult than yours.

The only difference between the people that overcome challenges and those that don't is having consistent influence over your focus.

What you focus on is what you're going to feel emotionally and physically.

You can change your focus by applying Kevin's rule....

Kevin's Rule

Every 60-days plan a trip, a hike, fishing expedition, or a long drive. Leave Friday night and return home Sunday morning.

If you're laughing because your husband or wife would never approve of you taking that much time for yourself, let them know that you'll be a better partner, parent, and leader if you take time to change the routine eight days a year. Extend the offer to them as well.

It doesn't have to cost a lot, but it should be memorable! Create memories with your closest friends or a leadership group—people that offer a different perspective. The only criteria is you should do something physical! Nothing can replace a memorable experience!

If it isn't scheduled it isn't real! It needs to become a requirement if our administrators are going to stay emotionally stable during these times.

HOW TO GIVE YOURSELF A MENTAL MASSAGE

MISOGI: a major event that marks your calendar year.

Schedule ONE big thing a year! Something truly challenging that you can be proud of yourself for. A long run, finishing a book, a 90-day commitment to health, a 30-day challenge—something that you can hang your hat on; something that no one can take away from you.

KEVIN'S RULE and a MISOGI were taught to me by one of my mentors, Jesse Itzler. He said as we age it becomes more important to play offense with your life. At the start of the year, schedule-in three trips with your closest friends and family. Schedule the rest of the year around your events. If you don't, you'll be playing defense throughout the year, doing everything for everyone else...

leaving no time to create memories with the people you love.

Scheduling fun and positive events that mark your year will give you something to look forward to and improve your mental health!

"BECOMING ORDINARY IS EASY. BECOMING EXCEPTIONAL REQUIRES WORK."

"YOU'LL NEVER BE HAPPY WITH YOUR BODY UNTIL YOU PRAISE YOURSELF FOR SOMETHING GOOD YOU'VE DONE."

II)
FOUNDATIONAL PRINCIPLES OF NUTRITION

WHEN YOU'RE IN ELEMENTARY SCHOOL, the last thing most kids are thinking about is a nutritional program.

Things change as you enter high school, college, your 30s, 40s, 50s—we keep changing.

Our desires change as well. Some of us want more energy, others need to improve focus, wanting to be as healthy and fit as we desire.

We always want to look good—and looking good can be defined in numerous ways. I will keep it simple: how we feel and see ourselves can determine how we feel about our overall health.

The good thing is, the foundational principles of nutrition are meant for everyone to follow. It doesn't matter how old you are, how healthy you are or aren't, or what the societal norms might be. The principles are the same.

The challenge is, there's so much noise around nutrition that you don't know who to listen to, or what program to follow, if any. Making things even more challenging is that when you do decide to take charge of your nutritional habits and begin your research, you'll find a contradiction for nearly everything being suggested.

I like to teach the foundational principles because they make sense!

Within each of these principles there are subcategories, meal plans, and training programs.

If you learn the principles, you can apply them to any nutritional program you desire.

Vegetarian, vegan, carnivore, plant-based, keto, pescatarian...The list is nearly endless.

Here are the three principles to help you build your lifelong journey in nutrition:

"WHEN YOUR 'WHY' GETS BIG ENOUGH, THE 'HOW' GETS SMALLER."

1) HYDRATION

The goal is to drink half your body weight in ounces daily. If you weigh 180 lbs, drink 90 ounces of WATER per day. Soda, sports drinks, energy drinks, and coffee don't count...It needs to be water.

After 8-10 hours of sleep (hopefully), your body will be dehydrated. The first thing the body needs is water. Drinking 32 oz of water will kick start your digestive system and fuel your thirsty cells that are seeking energy.

Our bodies are made up of more than 60% water, our bones are made up of more than 30% water, and your brain and heart consist of more than 70% water.

Your skin is the largest organ on the body, and it consists of more than 60% water.

Depriving your body of water will alter the functionality of your body.

If your goal is to lose weight, proper digestion and absorption of vitamins and minerals from food is unattainable if you're dehydrated.

If you aren't properly hydrated daily, your body doesn't burn fat and calories as efficiently.

When you aren't properly hydrated your energy will suffer. Instead of reaching for another energy drink loaded with artificial sweeteners and caffeine, drink a glass of water.

If you want to take it to another level, add a scoop of wheatgrass and make significant nutritional improvements, or add Ph drops to improve the alkalinity. Alkalized water helps the body regulate the acidic effects on the body from the environment and animal proteins.

When the body is properly alkalized with water and foods high in alkalinity, you don't have to use alkaline reserves within the body. When your body isn't using reserves to regulate from the effects of acid, your body burns calories more efficiently and will have more energy for the things you're passionate about throughout the day.

"PLEASURE IS ALWAYS DERIVED FROM SOMETHING OUTSIDE YOU, WHEREAS JOY ARISES FROM WITHIN." -ECKHART TOLLE

2) THE POWER OF AEROBIC FITNESS

Every nutritional program should have a section that explains the power of aerobic fitness. The primary function of training aerobically is to allow the body to burn fat for energy.

You develop aerobic power by training your body in your FAT

burning zone.

Generally, your fat-burning zone is when you're training in a way that allows you to have a conversation during your workout.

Scientifically, you can find your zone by following the example below:

Subtract your age from 220 and multiply that number by 0.5. This equals your aerobic fat burning zone.

For example, if you're 40 years old, subtract 40 from 220. The answer is 180.

Multiple 180 x 0.5

Equals = Heart Rate (HR) of 90 = Aerobic Fat Burning Zone

Based on the example above, your heart rate should be between 90-100 if you want to burn fat efficiently while you're training.

You should aim to train in your zone for 30-40 minutes daily, a minimum of 4-5 days a week.

"GUESS WHAT? YOU AREN'T THE ONLY ONE THAT DOESN'T HAVE IT FIGURED OUT."

Training out of your fat-burning zone is for cardiovascular development, which is also critically important. It's an entirely different form of training.

The healthiest way to train would be 30-40 minutes of aerobic training. Typically, a spirited walk or light bike ride.

You can add 15-30 minutes of anaerobic training with weights. Unfortunately, we have been led to believe that we have to deprive our bodies of food, exercise to exhaustion, and lift weights until we can't move the next day to lose body fat and get in shape.

It simply couldn't be further from the truth!

3) THE POWER OF DEEP DIAPHRAGM BREATHING

The fact that we don't teach kids to meditate or encourage them to meditate is mind-blowing to me.

ADHD is rampant due to poor nutritional habits and pharmaceutical influence through ads and our desire to have immediate satisfaction.

Anxiety amongst our teenagers and young adults is skyrocketing. The benefits of meditation are extensive, I'll highlight a few....

"STOP FEELING GUILTY. YOU AREN'T A VICTIM, YOU'RE THE VICTOR...LET IT GO!"

Meditation allows our body and mind to connect. Why is that relevant?

THE RICHEST BLOOD AND OXYGEN ARE IN THE LOWER ABDOMEN.

While you're meditating you're exposing the body to its richest natural source of energy and vitality.

THE HIGHEST ACHIEVERS IN THE WORLD PRACTICE MEDITATION...

Performers, speakers, world leaders, happy people, Tony Robbins, Michelle Obama, Ellen DeGeneres, Oprah, Tim Cook... all incorporate meditation, exercise, or other stress relief strategies into their daily routine, and they are intentional about their practices.

Achievement leaves clues!

If you don't have a meditation practice, here's a simple one...

Breathe into your abdomen for 2 seconds, hold it for 4 seconds and release it for 3 seconds. That's it.

Practice 15 of these deep diaphragm breaths 2 to 3 times a day. You'll improve your energy, mental clarity, and bring peace into your heart.

You can also practice meditation while active and moving by employing the same conscious breathing habits. Either way, ignoring one of the most sacred forms of creating peace within your body is going to hold you back!

I meditate daily—first thing in the morning, and any time I'm feeling overwhelmed and losing my focus.

RECAP: CREATING A KARLDANNY EDUCATOR

- Meditate daily. Most of the highest performers in the world have a meditation practice.

- Harness the power of aerobic fitness if you want to train your body to burn fat instead of sugar for energy.

- Hydrate and alkalize daily to maximize the body's ability to burn fat and have sustained levels of energy throughout the day.

- If you're confused about how to eat properly, YOU'RE NOT ALONE. There are contradictions for everything out there. The average person makes an impulsive decision on what to eat when they're confused. Following the simple guidelines in this chapter can ensure you stay on the journey of empowered health—not on the road to disease and illness.

"IT'S NOT WHAT HAPPENS TO YOU BUT HOW YOU REACT TO IT THAT MATTERS." – EPICTETUS

12)
RECOVERING FROM DEATH AND GRIEVING

OUR PARENTS AND CAREGIVERS TEACH US HOW TO LIVE.

Yet, oftentimes they don't teach us how to live when they're gone.

When you graduated from high school, things changed.

When you graduated from college, things changed.

When you got your first job, things changed.

As all of these things are changing for you, your caregivers are changing too. If you're fortunate to have grandparents, your time together has probably changed dramatically as well.

To make things even more challenging in the middle of all these changes, it's rare that our parents teach us how to adjust to one of the biggest changes in our lives...Living life without them.

My dad was a larger than life figure to me. Big, strong, fast, brave. When he passed on Christmas night (his favorite holiday), I had to reinvent myself and step into a role I didn't feel prepared for... how to carry on his legacy.

Over the years I have adopted this perspective...if you want to honor the people that have passed, practice an aspect of what you would describe as their legacy.

Perhaps it's kindness, sending thank you notes, singing on family vacations...choose something that makes you feel like their life was worth it.

When my dad moved on, I realized his legacy was unfinished.

Now it's my job to create the life he wanted our family to live in totality.

ACTION STEP:

Talk to your caregivers about what they want their legacy to be.

DID THEY JUMP:

I listened to Steve Harvey share his perspective on achieving the life you want—it's a great example of why some people live and some don't.

The hardest part is knowing that life has more to offer you—but you're going to have to jump to get it! When you jump, you may not know how far you're going to fall when you jump...but everyone has a parachute on their back! At some point, it's going to open!

If you want to see what's inside your parachute, you're going to have to jump. Everyone you know that has died, suffered, or supported you along the way has contributed towards your gifts.

Now it's your responsibility to jump—and never look back so your parachute can open. When it opens you'll see what gifts are wrapped up for you!

ACTION STEP:

Talk to your caregivers and find out if they jumped—ask if they took the leap toward what they envisioned for their life.

"FAITH IS THE ASSURANCE OF THINGS HOPED FOR, AND THE CONVICTION OF THINGS NOT SEEN."

PART A: GRIEVING HURTS

The first step in grieving death is asking yourself…did the person live fully while alive?

People that have fostered relationships, created experiences, laughed, cried, and taken responsible risks while they were on earth have a story to tell.

"SUFFERING IS A CHOICE, SO IS LIVING."

Those stories become your memories. Ultimately they will become your saving grace through grief.

The experiences you had with the deceased should be the first thing you focus on!

What they taught you…

The conversations you've shared…

The hard times you've overcome together…

The places you've traveled…

The personal touches they've given you that no one can ever take away...

Through their death, find peace in applying at least one thing that they taught you.

"THEY AREN'T COMING BACK. NOW CELEBRATE THEIR LIFE BY LIVING YOURS."

PART B: DOCUMENTATION

Early on, pictures and reminders of the deceased may hurt too much to look at. But frame them anyway—make sure your mementos and memorable events are kept together and preserved.

In time, those documented moments will become a treasure.

"I KNOW WE'RE RELATED BUT WE WEREN'T CLOSE."

If you discover that your estranged mother or father has passed away, and if you find yourself asking...

"Should I feel sad, hurt, or broken?"

"Do I need to go to the funeral?"

You get to choose if you're going to grieve, or NOT grieve!

If you feel as though you would like to recognize the deceased, it doesn't have to be in the traditional sense. No one has the right to tell you how to feel or how not to feel.

If you feel indifferent about recognizing the estranged, I still suggest you attend the funeral or burial service. You deserve to have the last word, leave your unanswered questions with the deceased, and grieve as you see fit.

Hopefully, this serves as a reminder that...

- You aren't wrong.

- They chose to not be in your life, and it isn't your fault.

- You couldn't have done anything to improve the relationship.

- You couldn't have done anything to heal the relationship.

- You couldn't have done anything to bring them back.

You only get one set of parents. Hopefully, you get to celebrate the life of both of them.

Regardless of what age you are, or the age of your parents when they transition, you may never be ready to let them go.

If you have a good relationship with your parents, part of the reason why letting them go is so hard is because you've never lived without them.

"IF IT WAS POSSIBLE TO LIVE WITH THEM, LIVE WITH THEM IN YOUR HEART AND YOUR ACTIONS."

Moving out doesn't count. Moving to another country doesn't count. Paying all your own bills and being independent doesn't count.

Living without them means...*you can't call them and hear their voice again.*

Living without them means...*you may feel alone for the first time in your life.*

Living without them means...*their job is done.*

When they transition, that reality hits people at different times.

Let go of the guilt. They're your parents—they know you loved them and they know you're sorry.

Embrace the mourning. It's time to put the lessons they've taught you into practice.

Celebrate their life by re-creating their favorite meal, enjoying their favorite glass of scotch, walking in the park they loved, playing the music that they loved, or attending their favorite sporting event.

Assume your place at the head of the table. Know that you're ready! You're ready because they've given you everything you need.

I can explain the stages of grief and the emotional roller-coaster you might be on...but it isn't going to solve everything.

My hope is after reading this section I've normalized your actions and emotions.

You may cry uncontrollably at times for years and years. Your heart may feel broken—but know it's normal.

The pain of not having them may never leave you, but you'll learn to live with it.

Please note: your grief is your own, but you aren't the first person to experience loss. It may feel that you're all alone, but you aren't. Tell someone that you're hurting.

THEY WILL FIND A WAY TO BE THERE FOR YOU.

"WHAT YOU RESIST WILL PERSIST...FACE IT." -CARL JUNG

RECAP: CREATING A KARLDANNY EDUCATOR

- Life is changing, so are your caregivers.

- Talk to your caregivers and ask if they made the jump towards the vision they had for their life.

- Talk to your caregivers and ask them what they want their legacy to be.

- Grieving hurts. You may never fully get over it—you learn to live with the pain.

- Celebrate their life by adding one thing they love to the life you're living.

- Hold onto mementos and documentation. One day you might be ready to reflect.

- Tell someone that you love and trust that you're hurting. They will find a way to be there for you.

"BE INSPIRED TO TAKE MASSIVE ACTION!"

TAKE MASSIVE ACTION

I STARTED QUESTIONING MY PERSONAL HISTORY when I started high school.

I wanted to learn about where I was from and who my great, great grandparents were.

I wanted to know why...

> *...the Black and Brown community didn't live in the suburbs I grew up in.*

> *...more Black athletes weren't exposed to the game of lacrosse—a game that has given me so much, and a community I'm proud to be a part of.*

> *...I feel so uncomfortable at times in a town that I love because my*

skin color is brown.

All of my unanswered questions followed me to college and remained unanswered—**UNTIL I PURSUED THE ANSWERS.**

When I started training athletes, I wanted to answer their questions.

"THE SECRET OF GETTING AHEAD IS GETTING STARTED." -MARK TWAIN

I certainly couldn't answer those kinds of questions as a trainer and as a teacher when I started. To overcome this, I kept notes on the most common challenges and put the work in to seek solutions to their challenges.

When I started to take notes, I started to really listen. I set out to find out what kids thought about—how they were really feeling; what experiences they dreaded and looked forwarded to.

When I started asking questions, I discovered high school and college-aged students—regardless of their background, race, gender, socioeconomic home life—all had the same basic questions, fears, and concerns.

Not only were they being left unanswered, but the kids also weren't even asking anyone the questions.

They were becoming robotic just to get through the day at school.

SAME routine, SAME books, SAME lectures, SAME tests.

After working with thousands of kids and families, I started to recognize similar patterns arising.

My ability to anticipate the road ahead as they went through high school and college made me a commodity that parents and kids wanted in their life.

Now I enjoy the conversations more than the training.

Knowing that those kids were going to need guidance, I dug in and armed myself with knowledge.

I have read countless self-help books, listened to podcasts daily, watched online videos of the greatest leaders and speakers of our time, prayed for guidance, and learned how to meditate to help me find the answers I knew the girls and guys I taught and coached were going to need.

I didn't want them to be like me when I left high school: proud of my diploma, the town I represented, and our accomplishments.

Back then, I was left so thirsty for knowledge about questions that no one ever asked if I was curious about. I was left asking myself after 13 years of schooling, *"Where do I start to look for the answers?"* I don't want you—or your kids—to have the same challenge.

"THE WILL TO WIN, THE DESIRE TO SUCCEED, THE URGE TO REACH YOUR FULL POTENTIAL...THESE ARE THE KEYS THAT WILL UNLOCK THE DOOR TO PERSONAL EXCELLENCE." -CONFUCIUS

Our school system is broken. But rather than just calling it out, I would like to offer a solution—even if that means I have to start grassroots efforts through a book like this.

I can help reform and transform the system we all rely upon to teach our kids how to launch into real life...

My prayer is...*that this book serves you and the educational institutions you rely on.*

We need to start having *different conversations* in the classroom and on the athletic field.

It isn't enough for a coach *to just be a coach!*

It isn't enough for a trainer *to just train!*

It isn't enough for a teacher *to just teach!*

It isn't enough for school administrators *to just be in charge!*

It isn't enough for our school boards *to just lead!*

It isn't enough if parents think *the school system is solely responsible for the personal development and education of their kids.*

"DO THE DIFFICULT THINGS WHILE THEY ARE EASY AND DO THE GREAT THINGS WHILE THEY ARE SMALL. A JOURNEY OF A THOUSAND MILES MUST BEGIN WITH A SINGLE STEP." -LAO TZU

EVERYONE HAS TO PLAY A BIGGER ROLE IN THE DEVELOPMENT OF OUR KIDS.

We can start by pouring into the spirits of our educators— investing in their personal development by sharing the 12 things outlined in this book. We have beautiful educators that have the talent, creativity, and desire to do deep work with our students.

We need leadership on the local level to empower our teachers by providing training—while being patient and strong enough to weather the storm of criticism as we embark on a NEW form of personal development (PD DAYS).

It's time to take action and change our school curriculum at the local and state level.

Adapt to the needs of our kids.

Take responsible risks.

Be more vulnerable in the process.

Ask uncomfortable questions.

Have the courage to say, 'I don't know' and seek the answers.

Have enough love in our hearts to ask for HELP!

I hope this book can be used as a springboard to finally address the most essential needs of our educators.

When we invest in our educators FIRST...

...they will have the power to change the communities, lives, and families they interact with daily.

Let's GO!

And as always...

BE INSPIRED TO TAKE MASSIVE ACTION!

BOOK RECOMMENDATIONS FOR OUR HIGH SCHOOL STUDENTS AND EDUCATIONAL LEADERSHIP TO SHARE

Stamped by Jason Reynolds

Tools of Titans by Tim Ferriss

Can't Hurt Me by David Goggins

Living With A Seal by Jesse Itzler

The Self-Compassionate Teen by Karen Bluth

Your Life Your Way by Joseph V. Ciarrochi and Louise L. Hayes

The Warrior Challenge by John Beede and Johnny Dombrowski

"LEADERS MUST BE CLOSE ENOUGH TO RELATE TO OTHERS, BUT FAR ENOUGH AHEAD TO MOTIVATE THEM." -JOHN C. MAXWELL

ABOUT THE AUTHOR

Rob is an educational consultant, husband, proud father of four, lacrosse coach, and fitness fanatic.

He has more than 15 years of experience as a classroom teacher and 20 years of experience as a personal trainer, speaker, and consultant.

Rob's work as a consultant focuses on healing the spirits of our educators. Rob believes our educators are breaking, but they aren't broken!

He has always stood by the belief his dad taught him:

When you see an issue, you have two choices...

"BECOME PART OF THE PROBLEM, OR PART OF THE SOLUTION."

If we choose to ignore the issue, we're becoming part of the problem. My hope is that *The 12 Things They Wanted to Teach You in High School...But Couldn't* becomes part of the solution for our high school educators around the world.

ACCOMPLISHMENTS:

NY State High School Lacrosse Coach of The Year

Who's Who of Personal Trainers

Award Winning Division 1 Football Player

50-Mile Ultra Runner

2x Collegiate Champion

3x High School State Champion

Founder of WinByDesign.co

Master's Degree in Education

Undergraduate Degree in Sociology and Physiology

Certified Athletic Performance Trainer

Certified Sports Nutritionist

Certified Health Coach

Be Inspired to Take Imperfect Action!

visit www.winbydesign.co

#rajrmethod #12thingsthebook